MALTA

TRAVEL GUIDE 2023

"Discover the Jewel of the Mediterranean: Your Ultimate Malta Adventure

JACKSON COLE

TABLE OF CONTENT

CHAPTER 1
INTRODUCTION TO MALTA

Welcome to the captivating island nation of Malta, where history, culture, and natural beauty converge to create an unforgettable travel experience. Nestled in the heart of the Mediterranean Sea, this small archipelago boasts a rich tapestry of ancient civilizations, breathtaking landscapes, and a warm, welcoming spirit that will leave you enchanted.

Step foot on Maltese soil, and you'll find yourself immersed in a living museum, where the whispers of the past echo through its majestic cities, towns, and archaeological sites. From the fortified walls of Valletta, a UNESCO World Heritage site and Europe's smallest capital, to the ancient city of Mdina, known as the "Silent City," Malta's history unfolds before your very eyes. Trace the footsteps of the Knights of St. John, explore millennia-old temples, and marvel at the engineering marvels of ancient civilizations.

Beyond its historical allure, Malta's natural wonders beckon with their awe-inspiring beauty. Picture yourself diving into the azure waters, exploring hidden caves, and encountering vibrant marine life. Discover the stunning cliffs and golden beaches that dot the coastline, offering a haven for relaxation and adventure seekers alike. Hike through rolling hills, traverse rural landscapes, and witness the rugged grandeur of the Maltese countryside.

But Malta is not just a land of tangible beauty. It is a land of warm smiles and genuine hospitality. The Maltese people, known for their friendliness and genuine warmth, will welcome you with open arms, inviting you to become a part of their vibrant community. Engage in lively conversations, savor traditional cuisine bursting with Mediterranean flavors, and partake in colorful cultural festivities that bring the island to life.

As you journey through Malta, prepare to be transported to a realm where time seems to stand still. Lose yourself in the labyrinthine streets, where history whispers its secrets. Witness the hues of the Mediterranean sunset paint the horizon in a symphony of colors. Immerse yourself in the island's rich tapestry of art, music, and folklore, and discover the spirit that defines Malta.

This is more than just a destination; it is an encounter with a land that embodies the essence of Mediterranean splendor. From the grandeur of its historical treasures to the untouched natural landscapes, Malta is a treasure trove waiting to be discovered. So, embark on this journey with an open heart and an insatiable sense of wonder, for Malta awaits, ready to captivate and inspire you in ways you never imagined possible.

OVERVIEW OF MALTA

Located in the central Mediterranean Sea, Malta is a small archipelago consisting of three main islands: Malta, Gozo, and Comino. This charming nation holds a unique position, blending influences from various civilizations that have left their mark on its history, culture, and architecture.

Geographically, Malta is situated south of Sicily, Italy, and north of the coast of North Africa. Its strategic location has made it a crossroads of civilizations throughout the centuries, with Phoenicians, Romans, Moors, Normans, Knights of St. John, French, and British all leaving their indelible imprints.

Malta's landscape is characterized by rolling hills, rugged cliffs, and picturesque harbors. The islands boast a mild Mediterranean climate with hot, dry summers and mild winters, making it an appealing destination year-round.

The capital city of Malta is Valletta, a UNESCO World Heritage site and a living testament to the island's rich history. Valletta showcases a harmonious blend of Baroque, Mannerist, and Neo-Classical architecture, with its stunning fortifications, grand palaces, and ornate churches. The city is also home to St. John's Co-Cathedral, a masterpiece of Baroque art and a must-visit attraction.

Gozo, the second-largest island in the archipelago, offers a more relaxed and rural atmosphere. It is renowned for its idyllic countryside, quaint villages, and scenic coastal views. The Azure Window, a natural limestone arch that once graced the island's coastline, sadly collapsed in 2017, but Gozo still enchants visitors with its serene beauty.

Comino, the smallest of the three main islands, is a tranquil paradise. It is famous for the Blue Lagoon, a stunning turquoise inlet surrounded by white cliffs and crystal-clear waters. Comino is an ideal spot for swimming, snorkeling, and diving, as its waters teem with vibrant marine life and underwater caves.

Malta's cultural heritage is deeply ingrained in its people, traditions, and way of life. The Maltese language, a unique blend of Semitic, Italian, and English influences, reflects this diversity. The island's rich cultural calendar is filled with vibrant festivities, including religious processions, village feasts, and traditional music and dance performances.

In recent years, Malta has also emerged as a thriving hub for arts and entertainment. The capital city hosts various cultural events, including international music festivals, theatrical performances, and art exhibitions.

Beyond its cultural and historical treasures, Malta offers a wealth of outdoor activities. From exploring ancient temples and fortresses to indulging in water sports and hiking along coastal trails, there is something for every adventurer.

Malta's warm hospitality, breathtaking landscapes, and vibrant cultural scene make it a destination that captures the hearts of travelers. Whether you seek a journey through history, a beachside retreat, or an immersive cultural experience, Malta promises to exceed your expectations and leave an indelible impression on your soul.

HISTORY OF MALTA

The history of Malta is a captivating narrative that spans over 7,000 years, making it one of the world's oldest inhabited locations. From ancient civilizations to colonial rule, Malta's historical journey is marked by the influences of numerous powers that shaped its culture, architecture, and identity.

Prehistoric Times:
Malta's earliest known settlers arrived around 5,200 BC, during the Neolithic period. These prehistoric people left behind a remarkable legacy in the form of megalithic temples, such as Ħaġar Qim and Mnajdra. These temples, believed to be the oldest freestanding structures in the world, are a testament to Malta's advanced civilization and their religious beliefs.

Phoenician and Roman Rule:

Around 800 BC, Phoenician traders established a presence in Malta, bringing with them their language, commerce, and maritime expertise. The Phoenicians were eventually succeeded by the Carthaginians and later, in 218 BC, Malta fell under Roman control. During the Roman era, the islands flourished economically and culturally, with the construction of impressive buildings and infrastructure.

Byzantine and Arab Rule:

In 533 AD, the Byzantine Empire conquered Malta and ruled for almost 300 years. However, in 870 AD, the Arab conquest reshaped the island's destiny. Under Arab rule, Malta witnessed an era of prosperity, scientific advancements, and the introduction of Islamic influences. The Arabs left a significant impact on Malta's language, agriculture, and architecture.

Norman and Knights of St. John:

In 1091, Norman forces under Count Roger I of Sicily captured Malta from the Arabs, beginning a new era of European influence. In 1530, the islands were gifted by Holy Roman Emperor Charles V to the Knights Hospitaller, a military religious order, in recognition of their service against the Ottoman Empire. The Knights of St. John transformed Malta into a formidable fortress, constructing fortified cities, such as Valletta, and defending against numerous Ottoman sieges.

The Great Siege and French Occupation:
One of the most notable events in Maltese history is the Great Siege of Malta in 1565, when the Ottoman Empire launched a massive assault on the island. The Knights, aided by local Maltese defenders, successfully repelled the siege, securing their status as heroic figures in Maltese folklore. However, in 1798, Malta fell to French forces under Napoleon Bonaparte, who ruled for a brief period before being expelled by the British.

British Colonial Rule:

From 1800 to 1964, Malta was under British colonial rule, serving as a strategic naval base in the Mediterranean. During this time, Malta experienced significant social and economic changes, including the modernization of infrastructure, the establishment of a British-style education system, and the growth of trade and industry.

Independence and Modern Malta:

On September 21, 1964, Malta gained independence from Britain, becoming a constitutional monarchy and later a republic. The country faced various political and economic challenges in the following years, but managed to establish a stable democracy and diversify its economy.

In 2004, Malta joined the European Union, marking a new chapter in its history as part of a larger European community. Today, Malta continues to thrive as a tourist destination, with its rich historical and cultural heritage, stunning landscapes, and warm Mediterranean charm attracting visitors from around the world.

The history of Malta is a testament to the resilience and adaptability of its people, who have embraced diverse influences and forged a unique national identity. From its prehistoric temples to its medieval fortresses and cosmopolitan cities, Malta's historical tapestry offers a captivating journey through time.

GEOGRAPHICAL FEATURES

Malta, a small archipelago located in the central Mediterranean Sea, is renowned for its stunning landscapes, rugged coastlines, and unique geological formations. Despite its relatively small size, the islands of Malta, Gozo, and Comino boast diverse geographical features that contribute to their natural beauty.

Islands and Coastline:
The Maltese archipelago consists of several islands, with the three main ones being Malta, Gozo, and 5Comino. Malta, the largest island, is characterized by rolling hills, rocky cliffs, and picturesque harbors. Gozo, the second-largest island, offers a more rural and tranquil setting, with idyllic countryside, fertile valleys, and sandy beaches. Comino, the smallest island, is renowned for its crystal-clear waters and the Blue Lagoon, a stunning natural inlet surrounded by limestone cliffs.

Cliffs and Rock Formations:

Malta's coastline is marked by dramatic cliffs and impressive rock formations, adding to its scenic beauty. The Dingli Cliffs, located on the western coast of Malta, provide breathtaking views of the Mediterranean Sea from their sheer limestone drop-offs. The Azure Window, a famous natural limestone arch on Gozo, sadly collapsed in 2017 but remains a symbol of Malta's geological wonders.

Beaches and Bays:

Malta is known for its picturesque beaches and secluded bays. Golden Bay and Mellieħa Bay on the northwest coast of Malta are popular sandy beaches, offering ample space for sunbathing and water sports. The Blue Grotto, a series of sea caves on the southern coast of Malta, enchants visitors with its vibrant blue waters and limestone formations.

Valleys and Countryside:

Inland, Malta boasts charming valleys and fertile countryside. Wied il-Għasri, located on Gozo, is a picturesque valley that leads to a secluded pebble beach. The picturesque landscapes and terraced fields of the Maltese countryside create a scenic backdrop, especially during the spring when the fields are in bloom.

Natural Reserves and Parks:
Malta is home to various natural reserves and parks that preserve its unique flora and fauna. Buskett Gardens, a small woodland on the outskirts of Rabat, Malta, offers a peaceful retreat and is known for its diverse bird species. Additionally, the island of Comino is largely uninhabited and serves as a nature reserve, providing a sanctuary for numerous bird species and other wildlife.

Underwater Caves and Marine Life:
The surrounding Mediterranean Sea offers a wealth of underwater beauty. Malta is renowned for its underwater caves, such as the Blue Hole on Gozo

and the Santa Maria Caves on Comino, attracting divers and snorkelers from around the world. The clear waters teem with vibrant marine life, including colorful fish, octopuses, and even the occasional dolphin or turtle.

Malta's geographical features showcase a diverse and captivating landscape. From the rugged cliffs and pristine beaches to the charming valleys and underwater caves, the archipelago offers a paradise for nature enthusiasts, outdoor adventurers, and those seeking tranquility amidst breathtaking scenery.

CLIMATE AND WEATHER

Malta enjoys a Mediterranean climate characterized by mild, wet winters and hot, dry summers, making it an inviting destination for tourists throughout the year. The islands of Malta, Gozo, and Comino experience pleasant weather with an abundance of sunshine and a relatively mild winter season.

Summer (June to August):
Summers in Malta are hot, dry, and sunny, with average temperatures ranging from 25°C to 35°C (77°F to 95°F). The sun shines for approximately 12 to 14 hours a day, providing ample opportunity for outdoor activities and sunbathing. Cooling sea breezes offer some relief from the heat, particularly along the coast. It is the peak tourist season, with the beaches and tourist sites bustling with activity.

Spring (March to May) and Autumn (September to November):

Spring and autumn in Malta offer mild and pleasant weather, with temperatures ranging from 15°C to 25°C (59°F to 77°F). These seasons are characterized by more moderate temperatures, fewer crowds, and a lush, green landscape. It is an ideal time for exploring the islands, engaging in outdoor activities, and enjoying cultural events and festivals.

Winter (December to February):
Winters in Malta are relatively mild compared to many other European destinations. The average temperatures range from 10°C to 15°C (50°F to 59°F) during the day. While it is the wettest season, rainfall is still moderate, and the sun often breaks through the clouds. Winter is a quieter period for tourism, but the island's historical sites and cultural attractions are still open and can be explored without the crowds.

Sea Temperature:

The Mediterranean Sea surrounding Malta remains warm throughout the summer and into the early autumn months, with temperatures reaching around 25°C to 27°C (77°F to 81°F). During winter, the sea cools down but remains relatively mild, with temperatures around 15°C to 17°C (59°F to 63°F).

It's important to note that weather patterns can vary from year to year, and occasional heatwaves or cooler spells may occur. It is always recommended to check the weather forecast before traveling and pack accordingly.

Overall, Malta's climate offers a pleasant and favorable environment for outdoor activities, sunbathing, and exploring its historical and natural attractions. With its abundant sunshine, mild winters, and warm summers, Malta provides an appealing destination for visitors seeking a Mediterranean getaway

CHAPTER 2
PLANNING YOUR TRIP TO MALTA

Planning a trip to Malta requires thoughtful consideration and careful preparation to ensure a smooth and enjoyable experience. This chapter will guide you through the essential aspects of planning your journey, including deciding the best time to visit, obtaining necessary travel documents, arranging accommodations, and exploring transportation options.

Choosing the Best Time to Visit:
Consider the climate and your preferences when determining the ideal time to visit Malta. The summer months (June to August) offer hot and dry weather, perfect for beach activities and outdoor exploration. Spring (March to May) and autumn (September to November) offer milder temperatures and fewer crowds, making it an excellent time to explore historical sites and enjoy cultural events. Winter (December to February) is

the quietest season, with mild temperatures and a chance to experience Malta's festive season.

Travel Documents:

Ensure you have the necessary travel documents before visiting Malta. Citizens from the European Union (EU) and the Schengen Area only need a valid national ID card or passport for entry. Non-EU citizens should check the visa requirements for their country of residence. It is advisable to have travel insurance that covers medical expenses and potential travel disruptions.

Duration of Stay:

Consider the length of your stay in Malta based on your interests and the activities you plan to engage in. A week is often sufficient to explore the main attractions of Malta, while an extended stay allows for a more in-depth experience, including visits to Gozo and Comino.

Accommodations:

Malta offers a range of accommodations, including luxury hotels, budget-friendly guesthouses, self-catering apartments, and charming boutique hotels. Consider your preferences, budget, and desired location when selecting accommodations. Popular areas to stay include Valletta, Sliema, St. Julian's, and Mellieħa, each offering a distinct atmosphere and proximity to attractions.

Transportation:

Malta has a well-connected transportation system that allows for easy exploration of the islands. Options include buses, taxis, car rentals, and ferries. Public buses serve most areas of Malta, offering an affordable way to get around. Taxis are readily available, but it's advisable to confirm fares before beginning your journey. Renting a car provides flexibility and convenience, especially for exploring rural areas and Gozo. Ferries operate between Malta and Gozo, providing a scenic mode of transportation.

Itinerary Planning:

Create an itinerary that includes the must-see attractions, historical sites, natural wonders, and cultural events that interest you. Some popular attractions in Malta include Valletta's historic sites, Mdina, the Blue Grotto, the Three Cities, and the Megalithic Temples. Plan enough time to relax on Malta's stunning beaches and enjoy the local cuisine.

Local Customs and Etiquette:

Familiarize yourself with the local customs and etiquette of Malta to ensure respectful interactions with locals. Maltese people are known for their warm hospitality, and it is customary to greet with a smile and a simple "hello" or "good day." When visiting churches or religious sites, dress modestly and observe any rules or guidelines.

By considering these aspects when planning your trip to Malta, you will be well-prepared to make the most of your visit and create cherished memories on this beautiful Mediterranean archipelago.

VISA AND ENTRY REQUIREMENTS

Before planning your trip to Malta, it's important to familiarize yourself with the visa and entry requirements to ensure a smooth and hassle-free journey. The specific requirements may vary depending on your nationality and the purpose and duration of your visit. Here is an overview of the visa and entry requirements for Malta:

Schengen Area:
Malta is a member of the Schengen Area, which is a zone comprising 26 European countries that have abolished passport control at their mutual borders. If you are a citizen of a country within the Schengen Area or a national of a country with a visa exemption agreement with the Schengen Area, you can enter Malta for tourist or business purposes without needing a visa. You will simply need a valid passport or national ID card to enter and stay in Malta for up to 90 days within a 180-day period.

Visa-Exempt Countries:

Citizens of certain countries, including the United States, Canada, Australia, New Zealand, Japan, and many others, can enter Malta without a visa and stay for up to 90 days within a 180-day period. This exemption applies to tourism, business, or visiting family and friends. However, it's important to note that the purpose of your visit should not involve employment or long-term stays.

Visa Requirements:

If you are a citizen of a country that is not visa-exempt, you will need to obtain a Schengen visa before traveling to Malta. The Schengen visa allows you to visit any country within the Schengen Area, including Malta, for a maximum duration of 90 days within a 180-day period. You must apply for the Schengen visa at the Maltese embassy or consulate in your home country or the designated visa application center.

The visa application process typically requires the following documents:

Completed visa application form
Valid passport with a minimum of six months' validity beyond the intended stay
Recent passport-size photographs
Proof of travel insurance with coverage of at least 30,000 euros for medical emergencies and repatriation
Proof of accommodation (hotel reservations, invitation letter from a host, etc.)
Proof of sufficient financial means to cover your stay in Malta (bank statements, sponsorship letters, etc.)
Round-trip flight itinerary
Purpose of visit (e.g., tourism, business, family visit)
It's advisable to apply for the Schengen visa well in advance of your planned travel dates, as processing times may vary.

Other Entry Requirements:

While not directly related to visas, it's important to note a few additional entry requirements for Malta: COVID-19 Restrictions: Due to the ongoing COVID-19 pandemic, there may be specific entry requirements, such as providing proof of vaccination, negative COVID-19 tests, or undergoing quarantine. Stay updated on the latest travel advisories and guidelines before your trip.

Return or Onward Ticket: It is generally recommended to have a return or onward ticket when entering Malta to demonstrate your intention to leave the country within the allowed timeframe.

It's essential to check the official website of the Maltese Ministry of Foreign Affairs or consult with the nearest Maltese embassy or consulate in your country for the most up-to-date and accurate information regarding visa and entry requirements.

By understanding and fulfilling the visa and entry requirements for Malta, you can ensure a smooth and enjoyable visit to this beautiful Mediterranean destination.

BEST TIME TO VISIT MALTA

Malta, with its Mediterranean climate, offers pleasant weather throughout the year, making it an inviting destination for travelers. The best time to visit Malta largely depends on your preferences, the activities you plan to engage in, and the type of experience you desire. Here's a breakdown of the seasons to help you determine the optimal time for your visit:

Summer (June to August):
Summer is the peak tourist season in Malta, characterized by hot and dry weather. Average temperatures range from 25°C to 35°C (77°F to 95°F), with the hottest months being July and August. This time is ideal for sunbathing on Malta's beautiful beaches, enjoying water sports, and exploring the crystal-clear Mediterranean waters. Summer also brings lively festivals and events, bustling nightlife, and a vibrant atmosphere.

However, be prepared for larger crowds and higher prices during this period.

Spring (March to May):
Spring in Malta offers mild and pleasant weather, making it an excellent time to visit for those who prefer fewer crowds and moderate temperatures. Average temperatures range from 15°C to 25°C (59°F to 77°F). The landscapes come alive with colorful wildflowers, and the countryside is green and picturesque. It's a great time for outdoor activities, such as hiking and exploring Malta's historical sites and charming villages. Additionally, spring brings various cultural events and festivals, adding to the cultural experience.

Autumn (September to November):
Autumn is another favorable season to visit Malta, with warm temperatures and fewer tourists compared to summer. Average temperatures range from 20°C to 28°C (68°F to 82°F) in September, gradually decreasing as the season progresses. It's a

perfect time for sightseeing, enjoying outdoor activities, and exploring the islands at a more relaxed pace. Autumn also marks the harvest season, offering opportunities to indulge in local produce and wines.

Winter (December to February):
Winter in Malta is mild compared to many other European destinations, making it an attractive choice for travelers seeking a winter getaway. Average temperatures range from 10°C to 15°C (50°F to 59°F) during the day. While winter is the wettest season in Malta, rainfall is still moderate, and the sun often breaks through the clouds. Winter is a quieter period for tourism, allowing for a more intimate exploration of Malta's historical sites, museums, and cultural attractions. It's also a time when you can experience the festive season with traditional celebrations and events.

It's important to note that weather patterns can vary from year to year, and occasional heatwaves or cooler spells may occur outside of the typical seasons. Before planning your trip, check the weather forecast and consider your preferences for crowd levels, activities, and overall atmosphere.

In conclusion, the best time to visit Malta depends on your preferences, but generally, spring and autumn offer milder temperatures and fewer crowds, making them favorable for outdoor activities and cultural exploration. Summer is ideal for beach lovers and those seeking a vibrant atmosphere, while winter provides a quieter and more immersive experience of the islands' history and traditions. Choose the season that aligns with your interests and enjoy the beauty of Malta throughout the year.

TRANSPORTATION IN MALTA

Getting around Malta is relatively easy, thanks to its well-developed transportation infrastructure. Whether you prefer public transportation, taxis, or renting a car, there are several convenient options available to explore the islands. Here's a comprehensive overview of transportation in Malta:

Public Buses:
Public buses are a popular and affordable mode of transportation in Malta. The bus network covers most areas of the islands, including major towns, tourist attractions, and the airport. The buses are operated by the Malta Public Transport (MPT) company, and they offer regular services throughout the day. Bus fares are based on distance and can be paid in cash or by using a contactless card. It's advisable to check the bus schedules and plan your journey in advance, especially during peak tourist seasons.

Taxis:

Taxis are readily available in Malta, and they provide a convenient and comfortable way to get around, particularly for shorter distances or when public transportation is limited. Taxis can be hailed on the street, found at designated taxi stands, or booked through taxi companies. Make sure to confirm the fare with the driver before starting your journey, as taxis in Malta do not typically use meters.

Car Rentals:

Renting a car is a popular choice for visitors who prefer the flexibility and independence of having their own transportation. Several car rental agencies operate in Malta, offering a wide range of vehicles to suit different needs and budgets. It's important to note that in Malta, driving is on the left-hand side, and traffic can be busy, particularly in urban areas. Make sure to familiarize yourself with local driving regulations, including speed limits and parking restrictions.

Ferries and Water Taxis:

Malta's strategic location in the Mediterranean Sea allows for easy access to neighboring islands and attractions through ferry services. Regular ferry services operate between Malta and its sister islands, Gozo and Comino, providing a scenic and enjoyable way to explore the archipelago. Additionally, water taxis offer an alternative mode of transportation, particularly for shorter distances or private transfers.

Walking and Cycling:

Malta's relatively small size and picturesque landscapes make it a favorable destination for walking and cycling enthusiasts. Many towns and cities have well-preserved historical centers that are best explored on foot. In recent years, efforts have been made to improve cycling infrastructure, with dedicated cycling lanes and rental services available in some areas. However, it's important to note that the roads in Malta can be narrow and busy, so caution should be exercised when walking or cycling.

Ride-Hailing Services:
Popular ride-hailing services like Uber and Bolt operate in Malta, providing an alternative transportation option. These services allow you to book a private driver using a mobile app, providing convenience and reliability, especially for longer journeys or when traveling with luggage.

It's important to note that the Maltese islands have a comprehensive transportation system, but traffic congestion can occur during peak hours, particularly in urban areas. It's advisable to plan your journeys accordingly and allow extra time for potential delays.

By utilizing the various transportation options available in Malta, you can easily navigate the islands and explore its diverse attractions, historical sites, stunning coastlines, and charming towns at your own pace.

CURRENCY AND MONEY MATTERS

When traveling to Malta, it's important to understand the local currency and money-related aspects to ensure a smooth financial experience during your trip. Here's a comprehensive guide to currency and money matters in Malta:

Currency:
The official currency of Malta is the Euro (€). It replaced the Maltese Lira (MTL) in 2008 when Malta joined the Eurozone. The Euro is divided into cents, with coins available in denominations of 1, 2, 5, 10, 20, and 50 cents, as well as 1 and 2 Euro coins. Banknotes come in denominations of 5, 10, 20, 50, 100, 200, and 500 Euros. It's advisable to carry a mix of smaller denomination notes and coins for convenience.

Currency Exchange:
Currency exchange services are widely available in Malta, including at banks, exchange bureaus, and

some hotels. Banks usually offer competitive exchange rates, and some may charge a small commission fee. Exchange bureaus and other private currency exchange services may have varying rates and fees, so it's advisable to compare rates before making an exchange. Avoid exchanging money at airports or tourist areas, as they often offer less favorable rates.

ATM and Cash Withdrawals:
ATMs (Automated Teller Machines) are plentiful in Malta and are the most convenient way to obtain local currency. They are available at banks, shopping centers, and other public areas. Most ATMs accept major international debit and credit cards, including Visa and Mastercard. Check with your bank before traveling to ensure your card will work overseas and inquire about any foreign transaction fees or withdrawal limits. Some ATMs may offer to charge your card in your home currency (Dynamic Currency Conversion), but it's

generally advisable to choose the local currency option to avoid additional fees.

Credit and Debit Cards:
Credit and debit cards are widely accepted in Malta, especially in hotels, restaurants, shops, and larger establishments. Visa and Mastercard are the most commonly accepted cards, followed by American Express and Diners Club. It's always advisable to inform your bank or credit card company of your travel plans to avoid any potential issues with card usage. Be cautious when using your card for smaller purchases or in more remote areas, as some establishments may prefer cash payments or have limited card acceptance.

Tipping:
Tipping in Malta is not obligatory, but it's customary to leave a small gratuity for good service. In restaurants, a 10% tip is commonly given if a service charge is not already included in the bill. For taxis, rounding up the fare or leaving a small tip

is appreciated but not mandatory. Tipping hotel staff, tour guides, and other service providers is at your discretion based on the level of service received.

Safety and Security:
While Malta is generally considered a safe destination, it's always advisable to take precautions with your money and valuables. Keep your cash, cards, and important documents secure, preferably in a money belt or a hidden pouch. Be cautious of pickpockets, particularly in crowded tourist areas, and avoid displaying large sums of money in public.

By familiarizing yourself with the currency, exchange options, and money-related practices in Malta, you can have a hassle-free financial experience during your visit. Enjoy your time exploring the beautiful islands and the rich cultural experiences they have to offer.

LANGUAGE AND COMMUNICATION

The Maltese archipelago has a unique linguistic landscape that reflects its rich cultural history. Here's a comprehensive guide to the language and communication in Malta:

Maltese Language:
The Maltese language is the national language of Malta and holds the status of an official language along with English. It is the only Semitic language written in the Latin script. Maltese has evolved from a combination of Arabic, Italian, Sicilian, and English influences, resulting in a distinct language spoken by the Maltese people. While Maltese is predominantly spoken among the locals, English is widely understood and spoken by the Maltese population.

English Language:
English is recognized as the second official language in Malta and is widely spoken and understood

throughout the islands. English has a significant presence in Malta due to its historical ties with the British Empire. Most Maltese people are bilingual, comfortably switching between Maltese and English in everyday conversations. English is commonly used in business, education, tourism, and official government matters. As a result, communication in English should not pose a significant barrier for visitors to Malta.

Communication for Visitors:
English is commonly used in hotels, restaurants, tourist attractions, and other places frequented by visitors. Signs, menus, and information boards are often available in both Maltese and English. Therefore, English-speaking travelers should have no difficulty communicating their needs and understanding the necessary information during their visit to Malta.

Basic Maltese Phrases:

While not necessary, learning a few basic phrases in Maltese can be appreciated by locals and can enhance your cultural experience. Here are some commonly used Maltese phrases:

Hello: Bonġu

Goodbye: Saħħa

Please: Jekk jogħġbok

Thank you: Grazzi

Yes: Iva

No: Le

Excuse me: Skużani

Sorry: Spiċċani

Where is...?: Fejn hu...?

How much does it cost?: Kemm jiswa dan?

Language Diversity:

In addition to Maltese and English, you may encounter other languages spoken by the multicultural population of Malta. Due to its geographic location and history, languages such as Italian, French, and German may be spoken by some residents or visitors. However, English remains the most commonly spoken foreign language.

Language Schools:
For those interested in learning or improving their language skills while in Malta, language schools are available throughout the islands. These schools offer courses in English and other languages, providing opportunities to immerse yourself in the local culture and enhance your language proficiency.

In conclusion, the linguistic landscape of Malta reflects its unique history and cultural diversity. While Maltese is the national language, English is widely spoken and understood, making communication convenient for English-speaking visitors. Learning a few basic phrases in Maltese can be appreciated but is not necessary for daily interactions. Enjoy your time in Malta, where language and communication will not be significant barriers to your exploration and cultural experiences.

CHAPTER 3

EXPLORING MALTA'S CITIES AND TOWNS

Malta is a vibrant destination with a diverse range of cities and towns that offer a blend of historical charm, architectural marvels, and picturesque landscapes. Each city and town in Malta has its own unique character and attractions to explore. Here are some of the top cities and towns in Malta that are worth discovering:

Valletta:

As the capital city of Malta, Valletta is a UNESCO World Heritage Site and a must-visit destination. This fortified city showcases a harmonious blend of historical and contemporary elements. Explore its narrow streets, admire the baroque architecture, and visit popular attractions like St. John's Co-Cathedral, Upper Barrakka Gardens, and the Grandmaster's Palace. Valletta also offers stunning panoramic views of the Grand Harbor and hosts cultural events, including the renowned Valletta International Arts Festival.

Mdina:

Known as the "Silent City," Mdina is a fortified medieval town with a rich history. Step back in time as you wander through its narrow, winding streets, characterized by impressive palaces and charming alleys. Visit St. Paul's Cathedral, admire the panoramic views from the city walls, and explore the fascinating Mdina Dungeons. Mdina's timeless atmosphere, with its quiet streets and captivating architecture, provides a unique experience.

Rabat:

Adjacent to Mdina, Rabat is a town steeped in history and religious significance. Explore St. Paul's Catacombs, which date back to Roman times, and visit the impressive Roman Villa, a well-preserved archaeological site showcasing beautiful mosaics. Don't miss a visit to the stunning St. Agatha's Catacombs and the renowned Church of St. Paul.

Rabat is also known for its traditional crafts, including silverware and lace-making.

Sliema:

Located on the northeastern coast, Sliema is a lively seaside town known for its fashionable shopping districts, thriving nightlife, and picturesque promenade. Enjoy a leisurely stroll along the waterfront, indulge in shopping at The Point or Tigne Point shopping malls, and relax at one of the many cafes or restaurants. Sliema also serves as a popular departure point for boat trips to explore the surrounding islands.

Marsaxlokk:

Famous for its colorful fishing boats and bustling Sunday fish market, Marsaxlokk is a charming fishing village located in the southeastern part of Malta. Immerse yourself in the vibrant atmosphere as you browse through the stalls selling fresh seafood and local handicrafts. Enjoy a leisurely seafood lunch at one of the waterfront restaurants and soak in the picturesque views of the traditional Luzzu boats.

Birgu (Vittoriosa):
Situated across the Grand Harbor from Valletta, Birgu is one of the oldest and most historic cities in Malta. Stroll through the atmospheric streets and admire the well-preserved medieval architecture. Visit the Inquisitor's Palace, Fort St. Angelo, and the Malta Maritime Museum. Birgu also hosts various cultural events, including the Birgu Fest, which showcases the city's history and traditions.

These are just a few examples of the cities and towns in Malta that offer unique experiences and cultural treasures. Each destination has its own allure, history, and attractions waiting to be explored. Whether you're captivated by the grandeur of Valletta, the serenity of Mdina, or the seaside charm of Marsaxlokk, Malta's cities and towns offer a delightful blend of heritage and modernity, inviting you to delve deeper into the country's captivating past and vibrant present.

VALLETTA

Valletta, the capital city of Malta, is a true gem that captures the rich history and architectural splendor of the island nation. This UNESCO World Heritage Site is a treasure trove of cultural and historical landmarks, stunning views, and a vibrant atmosphere. Here's a complete guide to exploring Valletta:

St. John's Co-Cathedral:
One of Valletta's most iconic landmarks, St. John's Co-Cathedral is a magnificent baroque cathedral renowned for its ornate interior. Admire the intricate marble work, gilded details, and Caravaggio's famous masterpiece, "The Beheading of St. John the Baptist." The cathedral also houses a museum showcasing religious art and artifacts.

Upper Barrakka Gardens:
Located on the highest point of the city's fortifications, the Upper Barrakka Gardens offer

breathtaking panoramic views of the Grand Harbor and the Three Cities. Take a leisurely stroll through the beautifully landscaped gardens, enjoy the serene atmosphere, and witness the firing of the Noon Gun, a traditional ritual.

Grandmaster's Palace:
Step into the opulent Grandmaster's Palace, which served as the residence of the Grand Master of the Knights of St. John. Explore the State Rooms adorned with tapestries and historical artifacts. Don't miss the Palace Armory, housing an impressive collection of arms and armor from the medieval era.

Valletta Waterfront:
Enjoy a stroll along the picturesque Valletta Waterfront, lined with colorful historic buildings that once served as warehouses. Today, this area is home to restaurants, cafes, and shops, offering a perfect spot to relax, dine, and enjoy the views of the harbor.

National Museum of Archaeology:

Immerse yourself in Malta's prehistoric past at the National Museum of Archaeology. Discover artifacts, including the famous "Sleeping Lady" figurine, that trace the island's Neolithic, Bronze Age, and Phoenician periods. Gain insight into Malta's ancient civilizations and their fascinating cultural heritage.

Fort St. Elmo:

Explore the formidable Fort St. Elmo, a star-shaped fortress guarding the entrance to the Grand Harbor. Visit the National War Museum housed within the fort, which showcases Malta's military history, including World War II exhibits. Take in panoramic views from the fort's ramparts and learn about the island's strategic significance.

Strait Street:

Known as Valletta's former red-light district, Strait Street has transformed into a vibrant hub of nightlife, cafes, and live entertainment venues. Experience the lively atmosphere as you explore the quaint bars, restaurants, and music venues tucked away in this historic street.

Valletta Markets:
Visit the open-air market of Merchants Street, where vendors sell fresh produce, local delicacies, and traditional crafts. Discover the vibrant local market culture and indulge in authentic flavors of Malta.

Festivals and Events:
Valletta hosts various cultural events throughout the year. The Valletta International Arts Festival, held in summer, showcases a diverse range of artistic performances, including music, theater, and dance. The Carnival, held in February, is a lively celebration with colorful parades, costumes, and street performances.

Valletta's compact size makes it easy to explore on foot, allowing you to soak up its architectural grandeur, vibrant culture, and fascinating history at every turn. From its stunning cathedrals and palaces to its picturesque gardens and bustling waterfront, Valletta is a city that offers a captivating blend of old-world charm and modern vibrancy. Explore its treasures, immerse yourself in its cultural delights, and create lasting memories in this remarkable capital city of Malta.

MDINA

Mdina, also known as the "Silent City," is a medieval walled town that takes you on a journey back in time. With its narrow streets, ancient architecture, and serene atmosphere, Mdina offers a unique and enchanting experience. Here's a complete guide to exploring Mdina:

Explore the Ancient Streets:
Step into the ancient streets of Mdina and immerse yourself in its timeless ambiance. The city's narrow alleys, adorned with traditional houses and imposing palaces, create a captivating atmosphere. Take a leisurely stroll and discover hidden courtyards, beautiful balconies, and charming doorways as you wander through the maze-like streets.

St. Paul's Cathedral:
Visit the grand St. Paul's Cathedral, a masterpiece of baroque architecture that dominates the city's

skyline. Marvel at its ornate interior, intricate marble work, and impressive artwork. The cathedral is dedicated to St. Paul, who is believed to have been shipwrecked on the island of Malta.

Bastion Square:
Enjoy panoramic views of the surrounding countryside from Bastion Square, located at the edge of Mdina's fortifications. This scenic viewpoint offers breathtaking vistas of the Maltese landscape, including neighboring towns and picturesque countryside.

Mdina Dungeons:
For a glimpse into the darker side of Mdina's history, visit the Mdina Dungeons. These underground chambers depict the harsh reality of the city's past, including tales of knights, prisoners, and historical events. Explore the interactive exhibits and learn about the intriguing stories that lie beneath the city's surface.

Vilhena Palace:

Discover the stunning Vilhena Palace, a majestic 18th-century building that now houses the National Museum of Natural History. Explore the museum's collection of local flora and fauna, fossils, and geological artifacts, providing insight into Malta's natural heritage.

Mdina Experience:

For a comprehensive overview of Mdina's history, visit the Mdina Experience. This audiovisual presentation takes you on a journey through the city's past, showcasing its architectural wonders, historical events, and cultural significance. Gain a deeper understanding of Mdina's heritage and the stories that shaped the Silent City.

Traditional Crafts:

Mdina is known for its traditional crafts, including glassblowing, pottery, and filigree jewelry. Visit the local artisans' workshops and witness these skilled craftsmen at work. You can even purchase unique handcrafted souvenirs as a memento of your visit to Mdina.

Fontanella Tea Garden:
Indulge in a delightful treat at the Fontanella Tea Garden, located on the bastions of Mdina. Enjoy panoramic views of the island while savoring delicious cakes, pastries, and refreshing tea or coffee. The charming ambiance and breathtaking vistas make this a perfect spot to relax and soak in the surroundings.

Events and Festivals:
Throughout the year, Mdina hosts various cultural events and festivals. The Medieval Mdina Festival showcases the city's medieval heritage, featuring reenactments, music, and traditional crafts. The Christmas season brings the enchanting Mdina Silent City Illuminated, where the city is adorned with festive lights and decorations.

Mdina's timeless beauty and tranquility make it a truly captivating destination. Its historical significance, medieval charm, and architectural wonders provide an immersive experience for visitors. Explore the silent streets, admire the magnificent cathedral, and soak in the unique atmosphere of this enchanting city. Mdina invites you to step back in time and create memories that will last a lifetime.

SLIMA AND ST. JULIAN'S

Sliema and St. Julian's are vibrant coastal towns nestled along the northeastern coast of Malta. Known for their picturesque waterfront promenades, bustling nightlife, and luxurious resorts, these neighboring towns offer a blend of relaxation, entertainment, and scenic beauty. Here's a complete guide to exploring Sliema and St. Julian's:

Sliema Promenade:
Embark on a leisurely stroll along the Sliema Promenade, a bustling waterfront promenade that stretches along the coast. Enjoy stunning views of the Mediterranean Sea, watch the boats sail by, and take in the lively atmosphere. The promenade is lined with restaurants, cafes, and shops, making it an ideal spot for dining, shopping, or simply soaking up the sun.

Tigne Point:

Visit Tigne Point, a modern waterfront development that features a shopping mall, cafes, and a waterfront plaza. Indulge in retail therapy at the various boutiques and international brands, catch a movie at the cinema, or savor a delicious meal overlooking the sea. Tigne Point also offers a picturesque marina and beautiful views of Valletta across the harbor.

St. Julian's Bay:

Explore the picturesque St. Julian's Bay, a charming harbor surrounded by restaurants, bars, and cafes. Admire the colorful fishing boats and yachts that dot the bay and enjoy the scenic beauty. The bay is a popular spot for leisurely walks, and you can even rent a paddleboard or kayak to explore the azure waters.

Paceville:

Discover Paceville, the bustling entertainment district of St. Julian's. This vibrant area comes alive at night with its numerous bars, clubs, and casinos.

Experience the vibrant nightlife, dance the night away, or enjoy live music performances. Paceville caters to a diverse range of tastes, offering a variety of venues and entertainment options.

Spinola Bay:

Visit Spinola Bay, a charming and picturesque harbor within St. Julian's. Take a stroll along the waterfront promenade and admire the traditional fishing boats known as "luzzus." The bay is surrounded by an array of restaurants, offering a great selection of seafood and international cuisines. Enjoy a romantic dinner overlooking the bay and soak in the tranquil atmosphere.

Love Monument:

Discover the Love Monument, an iconic landmark located on the waterfront in St. Julian's. This larger-than-life sculpture depicts a couple embracing and has become a popular spot for photos and romantic gestures. Capture a memorable moment against the backdrop of the Mediterranean Sea and the colorful fishing boats.

Balluta Bay:
Relax at Balluta Bay, a picturesque bay located between Sliema and St. Julian's. This sandy beach is ideal for sunbathing, swimming, and enjoying water sports. The bay is surrounded by cafes, bars, and restaurants, offering a perfect setting for a leisurely day by the sea.

Cultural Events:
Sliema and St. Julian's host various cultural events throughout the year. The Malta Jazz Festival, held in July, attracts renowned jazz artists from around the world. The Sliema Arts Festival showcases local artists and performers, while the St. Julian's Arts Festival celebrates the creativity and talent of the local community.

Sliema and St. Julian's offer a blend of coastal charm, lively entertainment, and stunning vistas.

Whether you're looking to relax by the sea, indulge in shopping and dining, or immerse yourself in the vibrant nightlife, these neighboring towns have something for everyone. Explore the scenic promenades, enjoy the coastal beauty, and create unforgettable memories in Sliema and St. Julian's.

GOZO AND COMINO

Gozo and Comino are two enchanting islands located just off the coast of Malta. Known for their pristine beaches, crystal-clear waters, and untouched natural beauty, these islands offer a tranquil escape from the bustling mainland. Here's a complete guide to exploring Gozo and Comino:

Gozo:

Azure Window (Dwejra):
Visit the iconic Azure Window, a natural limestone arch that once stood majestically on the coastline of Gozo. While the arch sadly collapsed in 2017, the site remains a popular attraction, offering breathtaking views of the rugged cliffs and the azure sea. Explore the nearby Inland Sea, a small lagoon connected to the open sea through a natural tunnel, and embark on a boat trip to explore the surrounding caves.

Victoria (Rabat):

Explore the charming town of Victoria, also known as Rabat, which serves as the capital of Gozo. Visit the Citadel, a fortified city perched on a hill, and enjoy panoramic views of the island. Discover historical sites such as St. George's Basilica, the Old Prison, and the Folklore Museum. Wander through the narrow streets lined with traditional houses and local shops, and experience the laid-back atmosphere of Gozitan life.

Ramla Bay:

Relax on the picturesque Ramla Bay, a stunning sandy beach known for its reddish-golden sand and crystal-clear waters. Unwind under the Mediterranean sun, take a refreshing swim, or explore the dunes and surrounding countryside. Ramla Bay also features historical sites such as Calypso's Cave, linked to the myth of Homer's Odyssey.

Xlendi Bay:

Discover Xlendi Bay, a scenic fishing village nestled in a picturesque bay on Gozo's southwestern coast. Enjoy the small sandy beach, go snorkeling or diving to explore the underwater world, or hike along the cliffs for panoramic views. Indulge in fresh seafood at the waterfront restaurants while admiring the charming atmosphere of this coastal gem.

Ggantija Temples:

Explore the Ggantija Temples, an extraordinary archaeological site that dates back to the Neolithic period, making it one of the oldest freestanding structures in the world. Marvel at the massive megalithic temples, which are believed to have served as places of worship and rituals.

Comino:

Blue Lagoon:

Experience the breathtaking beauty of the Blue Lagoon, one of Malta's most famous natural attractions. The crystal-clear turquoise waters, white sandy seabed, and surrounding limestone cliffs create a stunning tropical paradise. Spend the day swimming, snorkeling, and sunbathing, or take a boat tour to explore the nearby caves and hidden coves.

Santa Marija Tower:
Visit the Santa Marija Tower, a 17th-century coastal watchtower that stands on the highest point of Comino. Enjoy panoramic views of the island and the surrounding sea, and learn about the tower's historical significance in guarding the island against pirate attacks.

Santa Marija Bay:
Discover Santa Marija Bay, a secluded beach on the southern coast of Comino. Escape the crowds and enjoy the tranquil atmosphere as you relax on the sandy shore or go for a swim in the crystal-clear waters. This hidden gem offers a peaceful retreat and is perfect for nature lovers.

Comino Caves:

Explore the stunning sea caves that dot the coastline of Comino. Take a boat tour or kayak through the crystal-clear waters to discover these natural wonders. Marvel at the rock formations, swim in the hidden lagoons, and witness the mesmerizing play of light and shadow.

Gozo and Comino offer a serene and idyllic escape, where you can immerse yourself in natural beauty, relax on pristine beaches, and explore historical and archaeological treasures. Whether you seek tranquility, adventure, or a blend of both, these islands provide an unforgettable experience that will leave you with memories to cherish.

MARSAXLO KK

Marsaxlokk is a picturesque fishing village located on the southeastern coast of Malta. Known for its vibrant and colorful markets, traditional fishing boats, and fresh seafood, Marsaxlokk offers a unique glimpse into the island's maritime heritage. Here's a complete guide to exploring Marsaxlokk:

Sunday Fish Market:
Immerse yourself in the lively atmosphere of the Sunday Fish Market, the highlight of Marsaxlokk. Stroll through the rows of market stalls filled with an impressive variety of fresh fish, seafood, fruits, vegetables, and local products. Engage with the friendly vendors, haggle for the best prices, and savor the delightful aroma of traditional Maltese cuisine.

Fishing Boats and the Luzzu:
Admire the traditional Maltese fishing boats, known as luzzus, that line the Marsaxlokk Harbor.

These vibrant boats are painted in bright colors, featuring distinctive eyes on their prows, believed to ward off evil spirits and bring good luck to the fishermen. Capture postcard-worthy photographs of these iconic vessels, and witness the daily activities of the local fishermen.

Marsaxlokk Waterfront:
Take a leisurely walk along the Marsaxlokk Waterfront, lined with restaurants, cafes, and souvenir shops. Enjoy the tranquil views of the harbor, dotted with colorful boats, and indulge in freshly caught seafood at one of the waterfront restaurants. Savor local delicacies such as lampuki (dolphin fish) and other Mediterranean specialties while enjoying the sea breeze.

Marsaxlokk Parish Church:
Visit the Marsaxlokk Parish Church, dedicated to Our Lady of Pompeii. Admire the beautiful architecture, intricate stonework, and exquisite interior decorations. Take a moment for quiet

contemplation or attend a religious service to experience the spiritual side of Marsaxlokk.

Delimara Peninsula:

Embark on a scenic walk or drive along the Delimara Peninsula, located near Marsaxlokk. Enjoy breathtaking coastal views, rugged cliffs, and secluded coves. The area is known for its unspoiled beauty, making it a perfect spot for nature lovers and outdoor enthusiasts. Keep an eye out for the historic Delimara Lighthouse, which has been guiding ships since the 19th century.

Marsaxlokk Bay:

Relax on the sandy shores of Marsaxlokk Bay, a picturesque beach with clear waters and tranquil surroundings. Unwind under the sun, take a dip in the sea, or go snorkeling to explore the underwater world. Enjoy the peaceful ambiance and escape the crowds of larger tourist destinations.

Marsaxlokk Festivals:

Experience the vibrant festivals of Marsaxlokk, which celebrate the local culture and traditions. The most notable festival is the Feast of Our Lady of Pompeii, held in May, featuring religious processions, music, fireworks, and street decorations. The village comes alive with joyful celebrations, providing a unique opportunity to immerse yourself in Maltese festivities.

Marsaxlokk is a captivating destination that combines the charm of a traditional fishing village with the vibrancy of a bustling market. Explore the colorful markets, savor the freshest seafood, and soak in the tranquil beauty of the harbor. Whether you're a seafood lover, a photography enthusiast, or a culture seeker, Marsaxlokk will leave you with lasting memories of Malta's maritime heritage.

CHAPTER 4

TOP ATTRACTIONS IN MALTA

Malta is a treasure trove of historical sites, stunning landscapes, and cultural experiences. From ancient temples to picturesque coastlines, the island offers a diverse range of attractions that cater to every traveler's interests. Here's a complete guide to the top attractions in Malta:

Valletta:
Explore the capital city of Valletta, a UNESCO World Heritage site renowned for its rich history and architectural beauty. Visit the Grandmaster's Palace, St. John's Co-Cathedral, and Upper Barrakka Gardens for panoramic views of the Grand Harbor. Lose yourself in the narrow streets and discover charming cafes, shops, and museums.

Mdina:
Step back in time as you wander through the ancient city of Mdina, also known as the "Silent

City." Marvel at the medieval architecture, visit St. Paul's Cathedral, and enjoy breathtaking views from the bastions. Don't miss the Mdina Dungeons for a spine-chilling journey into the island's dark past.

Blue Grotto:

Embark on a boat trip to the Blue Grotto, a series of sea caves renowned for their mesmerizing blue hues. Marvel at the natural rock formations and crystal-clear waters, and take in the beauty of this unique coastal attraction.

Hypogeum of Ħal-Saflieni:

Delve deep into Malta's prehistoric past by visiting the Hypogeum of Ħal-Saflieni. This underground temple complex is a UNESCO World Heritage site and one of the world's most significant archaeological discoveries. Marvel at the well-preserved chambers, statues, and intricate carvings dating back over 5,000 years.

Megalithic Temples:

Discover Malta's ancient temples, which predate even the Egyptian pyramids. Visit the Ġgantija Temples on Gozo, the Hagar Qim and Mnajdra Temples in Qrendi, and the Tarxien Temples near Valletta. These megalithic structures showcase the island's rich Neolithic history and are a testament to its unique heritage.

Comino and the Blue Lagoon:

Escape to the pristine island of Comino and immerse yourself in the idyllic beauty of the Blue Lagoon. Enjoy swimming, snorkeling, and sunbathing in the crystal-clear waters surrounded by stunning cliffs and vibrant marine life. Explore the island's walking trails and discover hidden coves and secluded beaches.

Marsaxlokk Fishing Village:

Visit Marsaxlokk, a traditional fishing village famous for its colorful fishing boats, bustling market, and fresh seafood. Stroll along the waterfront, savor local delicacies at the fish market, and soak in the authentic charm of this picturesque village.

Popeye Village:
Step into the world of Popeye at Popeye Village, a film set turned tourist attraction located in Anchor Bay. Explore the charming village, watch entertaining shows, and meet beloved cartoon characters. Enjoy a day of fun for the whole family.

Dingli Cliffs:
Take in the breathtaking panoramic views from Dingli Cliffs, the highest point in Malta. Marvel at the dramatic cliffs plunging into the sea and enjoy a serene walk along the picturesque countryside. Sunset is an especially magical time to visit.

Golden Bay and Mellieħa:
Relax on the sandy shores of Golden Bay, one of Malta's most beautiful beaches. Explore the nearby

town of Mellieħa, with its quaint streets, historical sites, and stunning views from Mellieħa Bay.

These top attractions showcase the best of Malta's history, natural beauty, and cultural heritage. Whether you're fascinated by ancient civilizations, seeking breathtaking views, or simply looking to relax on stunning beaches, Malta offers a wealth of experiences that will leave you enchanted.

ST. JOHN'S CO-CATHEDRAL

St. John's Co-Cathedral is an architectural masterpiece and one of Malta's most significant historical and cultural treasures. Located in the heart of Valletta, the capital city of Malta, this magnificent Baroque cathedral is renowned for its lavish interior, intricate artwork, and rich historical importance. Here's a complete guide to exploring St. John's Co-Cathedral:

History and Architecture:
Step inside St. John's Co-Cathedral and be transported back to the 16th century. Built between 1573 and 1578 by the Knights of St. John, the cathedral served as the conventual church of the Order. The exterior facade, although modest, belies the opulent beauty that lies within. The cathedral's design is attributed to the Maltese architect Girolamo Cassar, who expertly combined Gothic and Baroque elements.

Interior Decorations:

Prepare to be awestruck by the grandeur of the cathedral's interior. Every inch of the cathedral is adorned with intricate artwork, gilded details, and exquisite craftsmanship. The marble floor, inlaid with tombstones of the knights, is a masterpiece in itself. Marvel at the ornate chapels, elaborately carved wooden choir stalls, and magnificent altarpieces.

Caravaggio's Masterpieces:

One of the most renowned attractions within St. John's Co-Cathedral is the presence of two masterpieces by the famed Italian artist Michelangelo Merisi da Caravaggio. Admire "The Beheading of Saint John the Baptist" and "Saint Jerome Writing" in the oratory of the cathedral. These paintings showcase Caravaggio's exceptional talent and mastery of chiaroscuro.

Oratory and Museum:

Explore the oratory, where the Caravaggio paintings are displayed, and immerse yourself in the intimate atmosphere of this sacred space. The adjacent museum houses a collection of religious art and artifacts, including precious tapestries, silverware, and liturgical vestments. Learn about the history of the Knights of St. John and their significance in Malta's cultural heritage.

Co-Cathedral Museum:
Visit the Co-Cathedral Museum, located just across from the cathedral, to further delve into the history and artistic treasures associated with St. John's Co-Cathedral. Discover a vast collection of religious art, including intricate gold and silver reliquaries, paintings, sculptures, and artifacts that showcase the artistic legacy of the cathedral and the Order of St. John.

Audio Guide and Guided Tours:
To enhance your visit and gain a deeper understanding of the cathedral's significance,

consider utilizing the audio guide or joining a guided tour. These resources provide informative commentary on the cathedral's history, architecture, and artwork, allowing you to fully appreciate the cultural and artistic significance of this magnificent structure.

St. John's Co-Cathedral is a testament to the grandeur and artistic prowess of the Knights of St. John. It stands as a symbol of Malta's rich history and cultural heritage. A visit to this extraordinary cathedral is a journey through time, offering a profound glimpse into the island's past and a truly awe-inspiring experience for visitors.

THE BLUE GROTTO

The Blue Grotto is a mesmerizing natural attraction located on the southern coast of Malta, near the village of Żurrieq. Renowned for its stunning rock formations, crystal-clear waters, and captivating blue hues, the Blue Grotto is a must-visit destination for nature lovers and adventure seekers. Here's a complete guide to exploring the Blue Grotto:

Boat Trips:
Embark on a boat trip to fully experience the beauty of the Blue Grotto. Hop aboard a traditional Maltese fishing boat, locally known as a luzzu, or a small motorboat, and set sail towards the grotto. Traverse the calm waters, passing by dramatic cliffs and hidden caves, before reaching the entrance of the Blue Grotto.

The Azure Window:

As you approach the Blue Grotto, witness the striking Azure Window, a natural rock arch that has become an iconic symbol of Malta. Marvel at the impressive limestone formation and capture breathtaking photographs against the backdrop of the Mediterranean Sea. The Azure Window offers a dramatic introduction to the wonders that lie within the grotto.

Exploring the Caves:

Enter the Blue Grotto and be prepared to be amazed by the vibrant blue colors that illuminate the cave walls and the crystal-clear waters below. As sunlight filters through the natural arches and reflects off the limestone, the cave is bathed in a mesmerizing blue glow, creating a surreal and magical atmosphere. Spend time exploring the various chambers and admiring the intricate rock formations sculpted by nature over thousands of years.

Diving and Snorkeling:

For those seeking a more immersive experience, diving and snorkeling opportunities are available in the Blue Grotto. Dive beneath the surface to discover an underwater world teeming with marine life and vibrant coral formations. Snorkelers can explore the shallow areas around the grotto, witnessing the beauty of the underwater ecosystem and the azure colors from a different perspective.

Nearby Attractions:

Combine your visit to the Blue Grotto with a trip to nearby attractions. Just a short distance away, you'll find the Hagar Qim and Mnajdra temples, ancient megalithic structures that offer a glimpse into Malta's prehistoric past. The nearby village of Żurrieq is also worth exploring, with its charming streets, traditional houses, and quaint restaurants serving delicious local cuisine.

Safety and Weather:

It's important to note that access to the Blue Grotto is weather-dependent. Strong winds and rough sea conditions can sometimes limit boat trips to the grotto for safety reasons. It's advisable to check weather conditions and consult with local boat operators before planning your visit.

The Blue Grotto is a natural wonder that showcases the beauty and power of Malta's coastal landscapes. Its mesmerizing blue waters and unique rock formations create an enchanting environment that captivates visitors from around the world. Whether you choose to explore the grotto by boat, dive into its depths, or simply take in the breathtaking views, a visit to the Blue Grotto is a memorable and awe-inspiring experience.

MEGALITHIC TEMPLES OF MALTA

The Megalithic Temples of Malta are a collection of remarkable archaeological sites that bear witness to the island's prehistoric past. These extraordinary structures, dating back over 5,000 years, represent some of the oldest free-standing stone buildings in the world. Here's a complete guide to exploring the Megalithic Temples of Malta:

Ġgantija Temples (Gozo):

Located on the island of Gozo, the Ġgantija Temples are a UNESCO World Heritage site and one of the most significant megalithic sites in Malta. These massive temples, built between 3600 and 3200 BCE, consist of two adjoining complexes, characterized by their colossal limestone blocks and intricate corbelled ceilings. Explore the archaeological park surrounding the temples, which provides insights into the religious and social practices of Malta's prehistoric inhabitants.

Ħaġar Qim and Mnajdra Temples (Qrendi):

Situated on the southern coast of Malta, the Ħaġar Qim and Mnajdra Temples are another UNESCO World Heritage site. Ħaġar Qim, built around 3600 BCE, features a series of interconnected structures, while Mnajdra, dating back to 3600-2500 BCE, comprises three temple complexes built in a stunning coastal setting. Marvel at the intricate stone carvings, altars, and mysterious fertility symbols that adorn these temples, and learn about their astronomical alignments that mark important celestial events.

Tarxien Temples (Tarxien):

Located near Valletta, the Tarxien Temples are a complex of four interconnecting structures dating back to 3150-2500 BCE. Explore the intricately carved stone blocks, animal-shaped altars, and mysterious spiral designs that decorate the temples. The site also includes an onsite museum where you can learn more about the temples' history and the rituals performed by Malta's prehistoric communities.

Hypogeum of Ħal-Saflieni (Paola):
While not technically a temple, the Hypogeum of Ħal-Saflieni is an extraordinary underground complex that shouldn't be missed. This UNESCO World Heritage site is a subterranean structure dating back to 3600-2500 BCE. Descend into the chambers carved out of limestone and marvel at the intricate architecture, including the Oracle Room and the Hall of the Holy of Holies. The Hypogeum provides a fascinating glimpse into the beliefs and burial practices of Malta's prehistoric inhabitants.

Museum of Archaeology (Valletta):
To further enhance your understanding of the Megalithic Temples and Malta's prehistory, visit the Museum of Archaeology in Valletta. The museum houses a remarkable collection of artifacts, including pottery, tools, and religious objects discovered at various megalithic sites. Gain insights

into the daily lives, rituals, and cultural practices of Malta's early inhabitants through these archaeological treasures.

The Megalithic Temples of Malta stand as a testament to the island's ancient heritage and the architectural prowess of its prehistoric communities. These awe-inspiring structures provide a glimpse into a time long past and offer a unique opportunity to explore the mysteries and marvels of Malta's megalithic past. A visit to these extraordinary sites is an immersive journey into the island's rich history and a chance to connect with the ancient civilizations that once thrived on its shores.

THE THREE CITIES

The Three Cities, also known as Cottonera, are a trio of historic harbor towns located across the Grand Harbor from Valletta, the capital city of Malta. Comprising Vittoriosa (Birgu), Senglea (Isla), and Cospicua (Bormla), these enchanting towns are steeped in history and offer a glimpse into Malta's maritime past. Here's a complete guide to exploring the Three Cities:

Vittoriosa (Birgu):
Vittoriosa, the oldest of the Three Cities, is a fortified town that served as the first home of the Knights of St. John upon their arrival in Malta. Walk through the narrow, winding streets lined with medieval buildings and admire the well-preserved architecture. Visit the imposing Fort St. Angelo, which played a crucial role in the Great Siege of Malta. Explore the Maritime Museum and Inquisitor's Palace to learn more about the town's

maritime heritage and its importance during the rule of the Knights.

Senglea (Isla):

Senglea, located on a small peninsula, offers panoramic views of the Grand Harbor. Known as the "Civitas Invicta" (Unconquered City), it played a vital role in the defense of Malta during the Great Siege. Stroll along the waterfront promenade, visit the impressive Fort St. Michael, and admire the picturesque streets lined with colorful houses. The Gardjola Gardens provide a perfect spot to relax and take in the breathtaking views of the harbor.

Cospicua (Bormla):

Cospicua is the largest of the Three Cities and was also heavily fortified to protect Malta from invasions. Explore the historic center with its charming squares, baroque churches, and grand palaces. Don't miss a visit to the stunning Collegiate Basilica of the Immaculate Conception, known for its elaborate interior and beautiful dome. The waterfront promenade offers picturesque views and is a popular spot for a leisurely stroll.

The Malta at War Museum:

Located in Vittoriosa, the Malta at War Museum provides a fascinating insight into Malta's experience during World War II. Discover the stories of bravery and resilience of the Maltese people as they endured relentless bombings and fought for survival. The museum showcases artifacts, photographs, and personal testimonies that offer a unique perspective on this tumultuous period in Malta's history.

Boat Tours and Harbor Cruises:

Experience the beauty of the Three Cities from the water by taking a boat tour or harbor cruise. Enjoy a leisurely cruise around the Grand Harbor, passing by historic fortifications, forts, and iconic landmarks. Boat tours provide a different perspective of the Three Cities, allowing you to appreciate their grandeur and maritime significance.

Festivals and Events:
The Three Cities come alive during various festivals and events throughout the year. One of the most renowned is the Birgu Candlelight Festival, held in October, where the streets of Vittoriosa are illuminated by thousands of candles, creating a magical atmosphere. The Three Cities also host cultural events, concerts, and traditional processions, providing a vibrant glimpse into the local traditions and celebrations.

The Three Cities offer a captivating blend of history, culture, and maritime charm. With their well-preserved architecture, fascinating museums, and panoramic views, these historic harbor towns provide a unique and immersive experience for visitors. Step back in time and explore the rich heritage of the Three Cities, and you'll discover a side of Malta that is both intriguing and enchanting.

POPEYE VILLAGE

Popeye Village, also known as Sweethaven Village, is a unique and picturesque tourist attraction located in Anchor Bay, on the northwest coast of the island of Malta. Originally built as a film set for the 1980 musical production of "Popeye," starring Robin Williams, the village has since been transformed into a charming theme park that celebrates the beloved spinach-loving sailor. Here's a complete guide to visiting Popeye Village:

History and Film Set:
Popeye Village was constructed in 1979 as a purpose-built film set for the production of the live-action musical "Popeye." The set was meticulously designed to resemble the fictional village of Sweethaven, Popeye's home. Today, visitors can explore the original film set, which has been preserved and restored to its former glory.

Themed Attractions:

Step into the world of Popeye and embark on a fun-filled adventure at the village. The colorful and whimsical houses, streets, and buildings create a nostalgic atmosphere, reminiscent of the classic cartoon. Enjoy a variety of attractions and activities, including boat rides, water trampolines, a mini-golf course, and a play pool with water games. Visitors of all ages can immerse themselves in the playful spirit of Popeye and his friends.

Popeye Shows and Performances:

One of the highlights of a visit to Popeye Village is the live performances and shows. Experience entertaining live shows featuring Popeye, Olive Oyl, and other beloved characters from the Popeye cartoons. Enjoy music, dancing, and comedic acts that bring the village to life. Interactive experiences and meet-and-greet sessions with the characters offer a memorable experience for both children and adults.

Museum and Exhibitions:

Learn about the history of Popeye and the making of the film at the onsite Popeye Museum. Discover fascinating behind-the-scenes information, original props, and memorabilia from the movie production. Interactive displays and exhibitions provide insights into the creative process and the impact of Popeye on popular culture.

Souvenir Shops and Dining:

Explore the village's souvenir shops, which offer a wide range of Popeye-themed merchandise, including t-shirts, toys, and collectibles. Indulge in a delicious meal at one of the village's restaurants, serving Mediterranean and Maltese cuisine. Relax and enjoy the beautiful views of Anchor Bay while savoring a taste of local delicacies.

Events and Festivals:

Throughout the year, Popeye Village hosts various events and festivals that add an extra layer of excitement to the visitor experience. From seasonal celebrations, such as Christmas and Halloween events, to special themed activities and performances, there's always something happening at Popeye Village.

Popeye Village is a delightful and whimsical destination that captures the imagination and brings the beloved cartoon characters to life. Whether you're a fan of Popeye or simply seeking a fun-filled day of entertainment, a visit to Popeye Village promises an enjoyable and nostalgic experience for the whole family. Immerse yourself in the vibrant world of Popeye, and you'll create cherished memories that will last a lifetime.

CHAPTER 5
OUTDOOR ACTIVITIES IN MALTA

Malta, with its stunning landscapes, crystal-clear waters, and pleasant climate, offers a wide array of outdoor activities for adventure enthusiasts and nature lovers alike. From exploring pristine beaches to embarking on thrilling water sports and enjoying scenic hikes, there's something for everyone. Here's a comprehensive guide to the outdoor activities you can enjoy in Malta:

Beaches and Water Sports:
Malta boasts numerous beautiful beaches where you can soak up the sun and swim in the inviting Mediterranean Sea. Golden Bay, Mellieħa Bay, and Ramla Bay are popular choices, offering soft sand and clear waters. For water sports enthusiasts, Malta offers an abundance of activities such as snorkeling, scuba diving, kayaking, paddleboarding, jet skiing, and windsurfing. Discover vibrant

marine life, hidden coves, and underwater caves as you delve into the waters surrounding the island.

Coastal Walks and Hiking:

Take advantage of Malta's scenic coastal paths and hiking trails that offer breathtaking views and a chance to explore the island's natural beauty. The Dingli Cliffs, located on the western coast, provide stunning panoramic vistas of the Mediterranean Sea. The Victoria Lines, a historic defensive fortification, offers a unique hiking experience, with paths winding through rugged terrain and ancient ruins. The picturesque fishing village of Marsaxlokk and the stunning Blue Grotto area are also great places to explore on foot.

Rock Climbing and Abseiling:

For adrenaline junkies, Malta offers excellent rock climbing and abseiling opportunities. Test your skills on the island's limestone cliffs and enjoy the exhilaration of scaling vertical walls while surrounded by stunning coastal scenery. Comino

Island's Santa Marija Caves are a popular spot for rock climbing, while cliffs in various locations, including Għar Lapsi and Wied il-Mielaħ, offer thrilling challenges for climbers of all levels.

Cycling and Mountain Biking:

Discover the beauty of Malta's countryside and historic sites on two wheels. The island features a network of cycling routes and trails, catering to both leisure cyclists and mountain biking enthusiasts. Explore scenic coastal roads, quaint villages, and off-road tracks that wind through picturesque landscapes. The island's relatively small size makes it easy to cover a lot of ground, and you can rent bicycles or join guided cycling tours to enhance your experience.

Boat Trips and Sailing:

Embark on a boat trip or sailing excursion to explore Malta's coastline and nearby islands. Cruise around the stunning Blue Lagoon in Comino, anchor in secluded bays, and enjoy swimming and snorkeling in pristine waters. Take a traditional Maltese fishing boat, known as a luzzu, to experience local maritime traditions and discover hidden gems along the coast.

Birdwatching and Nature Reserves:
Malta is a paradise for birdwatching enthusiasts, particularly during spring and autumn migrations. The island serves as a resting point for various species, and nature reserves like the Ghadira Nature Reserve in Mellieħa and the Is-Simar Nature Reserve in Marsaskala provide ideal locations for birdwatching. Explore these reserves to observe a diverse range of bird species, as well as other wildlife and native flora.

Horseback Riding:
Experience the beauty of Malta's countryside on horseback. Several equestrian centers across the island offer guided horseback riding excursions, allowing you to meander through rural landscapes, vineyards, and olive groves. Discover hidden trails

and enjoy breathtaking views as you connect with nature in a unique and peaceful way.

Golfing:

Enjoy a round of golf amidst stunning landscapes at one of Malta's golf courses. The Royal Malta Golf Club, located in the heart of the island, offers an 18-hole course set in a picturesque setting, while the Marsa Sports Club features a challenging 9-hole course. Both venues provide an excellent opportunity to combine sport with the natural beauty of the Maltese countryside.

Malta's outdoor activities allow you to immerse yourself in the island's natural wonders, from its crystal-clear waters to its rugged coastlines and picturesque landscapes. Whether you're seeking adventure, relaxation, or simply a connection with nature, Malta offers an abundance of opportunities to satisfy your outdoor cravings. So, get ready to embrace the island's playground and create unforgettable memories amidst its stunning natural surroundings.

BEACHES AND WATER SPORTS

Malta, with its pristine coastline and azure waters, is a haven for beach lovers and water sports enthusiasts. From sun-drenched sandy shores to hidden coves and rocky bays, the island offers a diverse range of beaches to suit every preference. Dive into the refreshing Mediterranean Sea, indulge in thrilling water sports, or simply relax and soak up the sun. Here's a complete guide to the beaches and water sports in Malta:

Golden Bay:
Located on the northwestern coast of Malta, Golden Bay is a popular beach known for its golden sands and crystal-clear waters. Surrounded by rugged cliffs and lush countryside, it offers a stunning backdrop for a day of sunbathing and swimming. The beach is equipped with facilities such as sunbeds, umbrellas, and beachside restaurants, ensuring a comfortable and enjoyable experience.

Mellieħa Bay:

Mellieħa Bay, also known as Ghadira Bay, is the largest sandy beach in Malta. With its shallow, calm waters, it's perfect for families with children. The beach is well-equipped with facilities, including water sports centers offering activities such as jet skiing, paddleboarding, and parasailing. Explore the vibrant underwater world by snorkeling or scuba diving, as the bay is home to a variety of marine life.

Ramla Bay:

Nestled on the northern coast of Gozo, Malta's sister island, Ramla Bay is renowned for its stunning red sand and turquoise waters. Surrounded by scenic countryside and hills, it offers a tranquil and picturesque setting. The beach is ideal for sunbathing and swimming, and you can also rent kayaks or paddleboards to explore the bay at your own pace.

Blue Lagoon (Comino Island):

The Blue Lagoon, located on the small island of Comino, is a breathtaking natural wonder. Its crystal-clear, turquoise waters are perfect for swimming and snorkeling. The lagoon's shallow depths and vibrant marine life make it an ideal spot for underwater exploration. Take a boat trip from Malta or Gozo to spend a day in this paradise-like setting.

St. Peter's Pool:

For those seeking a more rugged and secluded beach experience, St. Peter's Pool is a hidden gem located near Marsaxlokk in southeastern Malta. This natural swimming pool is carved out of limestone and offers a unique setting for swimming and sunbathing. The surrounding cliffs provide excellent diving opportunities for those looking to explore the underwater world.

Water Sports:

Malta's warm waters and favorable weather conditions make it a prime destination for water sports enthusiasts. Try your hand at thrilling activities such as jet skiing, water skiing, windsurfing, and parasailing. Numerous water sports centers and rental shops are available along the popular beaches, offering equipment and instruction for beginners and experienced enthusiasts alike.

Snorkeling and Scuba Diving:
Explore Malta's vibrant underwater world by snorkeling or scuba diving. The island boasts excellent visibility, diverse marine life, and fascinating underwater landscapes, including caves, reefs, and shipwrecks. Dive sites such as the Blue Grotto, Cirkewwa, and Santa Marija Caves in Comino offer incredible underwater experiences for both beginners and advanced divers.

Boat Trips and Cruises:
Embark on a boat trip or cruise to fully appreciate Malta's coastal beauty. Enjoy a leisurely cruise around the islands, visit secluded coves, and

discover hidden caves and rock formations. Some boat trips also include stops for swimming, snorkeling, and exploring specific attractions such as the Blue Lagoon or the caves of Comino.

Whether you prefer relaxing on sandy shores, exploring underwater wonders, or indulging in thrilling water sports, Malta's beaches and water sports scene have something to offer everyone. So, grab your swimsuit, sunscreen, and sense of adventure, and immerse yourself in the coastal beauty of this Mediterranean gem.

DIVING AND SNORKELING

Malta's crystal-clear waters and diverse marine life make it a paradise for diving and snorkeling enthusiasts. Whether you're a seasoned diver or a beginner looking to explore the underwater world, Malta offers a wealth of underwater sites, including vibrant reefs, fascinating caves, and historic shipwrecks. Here's a complete guide to diving and snorkeling in Malta:

Blue Grotto:
Located on the southwestern coast of Malta, the Blue Grotto is a must-visit destination for divers and snorkelers. This stunning natural formation consists of a series of sea caves, renowned for their vibrant blue hues. Dive into the clear waters and explore the caves' enchanting beauty, adorned with colorful marine life and intriguing rock formations.

Comino Island:

The island of Comino, situated between Malta and Gozo, is a haven for divers and snorkelers. The crystal-clear waters surrounding the island offer excellent visibility and a rich underwater ecosystem. The Santa Marija Caves and the Blue Lagoon are popular diving and snorkeling spots, teeming with marine life, including colorful fish, octopuses, and even seahorses.

Cirkewwa:

Cirkewwa, located on the northern coast of Malta, is a popular diving site known for its diverse marine life and underwater topography. Explore the reef formations and encounter a wide array of fish species, such as barracudas, groupers, and moray eels. The site also features the wreck of the P29 patrol boat, which was deliberately sunk to create an artificial reef and has become a popular attraction for divers.

Wied iż-Żurrieq:

Wied iż-Żurrieq is a picturesque inlet on the southern coast of Malta, famous for its stunning cliffs and the Blue Grotto cave system. Snorkelers can explore the crystal-clear waters and witness the captivating underwater scenery, including colorful coral formations and a variety of marine species.

Gozo:

Gozo, Malta's sister island, offers exceptional diving and snorkeling opportunities. The island is known for its dramatic underwater landscapes, including stunning arches, caves, and drop-offs. Dwejra Bay, home to the iconic Azure Window (until its collapse in 2017), was a popular diving site, and while the arch no longer stands, the area still offers remarkable diving experiences.

Underwater Caves and Wrecks:

Malta is also renowned for its captivating underwater caves and historic shipwrecks. The Santa Marija Caves in Comino, the Lantern Point Cave in Gozo, and the Billinghurst Cave in Malta are just a few examples of the remarkable cave systems awaiting exploration. For wreck diving enthusiasts, sites such as the HMS Maori and the Um El Faroud offer fascinating glimpses into Malta's maritime history.

Dive Centers and Courses:
Whether you're a seasoned diver or a beginner, Malta's dive centers cater to all levels of experience. Professional and certified dive centers provide equipment rental, guided dives, and dive courses, ensuring a safe and enjoyable diving experience for all. Qualified instructors are available to teach beginners the basics of diving, while experienced divers can participate in advanced training and specialty courses.

Snorkeling Excursions:
For those who prefer to explore the underwater world from the surface, snorkeling excursions are a fantastic option. Join a guided tour that takes you to the best snorkeling spots, providing equipment

and guidance along the way. Experienced guides will help you identify the marine life you encounter and ensure you make the most of your snorkeling adventure.

When diving or snorkeling in Malta, always remember to follow safety guidelines, respect the marine environment, and adhere to local regulations. Whether you choose to explore the captivating caves, swim alongside colorful fish, or uncover the secrets of historic wrecks, Malta's underwater wonders are sure to leave you with unforgettable memories of your aquatic adventures.

HIKING AND NATURE WALKS

Malta may be known for its stunning coastline, but the island also boasts breathtaking landscapes and scenic trails that are perfect for hiking and nature walks. From rugged cliffs and panoramic viewpoints to picturesque countryside and hidden valleys, Malta offers a diverse range of hiking experiences for outdoor enthusiasts. Lace up your hiking boots, grab your camera, and embark on a journey to discover the natural beauty of Malta. Here's a complete guide to hiking and nature walks:

Dingli Cliffs:
Located on the western coast of Malta, the Dingli Cliffs offer stunning panoramic views of the Mediterranean Sea. A leisurely walk along the cliff edge provides breathtaking vistas and a sense of serenity. Take in the vastness of the sea, enjoy the coastal breeze, and witness dramatic sunsets that paint the sky with vibrant colors.

Victoria Lines:

The Victoria Lines, a historic defensive wall stretching across Malta from east to west, offers a unique hiking experience. This scenic trail passes through picturesque countryside, rural villages, and ancient ruins. Enjoy the peacefulness of the surrounding nature as you traverse the hills and valleys, encountering historical landmarks along the way.

Buskett Gardens and Girgenti:

Buskett Gardens, located in the central part of Malta, is a wooded area known for its tranquility and natural beauty. Explore the shaded pathways and discover the diverse flora and fauna that call this area home. From Buskett, you can continue your hike to Girgenti, a charming rural village surrounded by vineyards and fields, offering stunning views of the surrounding countryside.

Majjistral Nature and History Park:

Majjistral Nature and History Park, located in the northwest of Malta, is a haven for nature lovers and hikers. The park features rugged cliffs, hidden coves, and scenic coastal trails. Follow the marked hiking routes to explore the park's diverse landscapes, encounter unique rock formations, and admire the rich biodiversity that thrives in this protected area.

Fomm ir-Riħ Bay:
For those seeking a more challenging hike, Fomm ir-Riħ Bay offers a rewarding adventure. This secluded bay, located on the western coast, can be reached via a steep and rocky path that descends from the cliffs. The effort is well worth it, as you'll be greeted by pristine turquoise waters and a secluded pebble beach, surrounded by dramatic cliffs.

Wied il-Mielaħ:
Wied il-Mielaħ, located near the village of Baħrija, is a picturesque valley offering a peaceful and scenic

hiking experience. Follow the winding paths through the valley, surrounded by lush greenery and towering cliffs. Admire the natural rock formations and enjoy the tranquility of this hidden gem.

Għar Lapsi:

Għar Lapsi, situated on the southwestern coast, is a popular spot for hiking and nature walks. The coastal trails provide stunning views of the rugged cliffs and the azure waters below. Explore the surrounding area to discover hidden caves, including the famous Blue Grotto, known for its captivating beauty.

Gozo Coastal Walks:

Gozo, Malta's sister island, offers exceptional coastal walks and hiking opportunities. The island's smaller size and unspoiled landscapes make it ideal for exploring on foot. From the breathtaking cliffs of Dwejra to the picturesque Xlendi Bay, Gozo's coastal trails provide a unique perspective of the island's natural beauty.

When embarking on a hiking or nature walk in Malta, it's essential to wear comfortable shoes, carry sufficient water, and follow any trail markers or signage. Respect the natural environment, take your time to soak in the scenery, and capture the beauty of Malta's landscapes with your camera. Whether you prefer coastal walks, countryside strolls, or challenging hikes, Malta's diverse terrain promises unforgettable outdoor adventures for all nature enthusiasts.

BOAT TRIPS AND CRUISES

Malta's stunning coastline, crystal-clear waters, and hidden gems make it an ideal destination for boat trips and cruises. Whether you want to relax on a leisurely cruise, explore secluded coves, or discover fascinating sea caves, there are plenty of options to choose from. Embark on a maritime adventure and immerse yourself in the coastal splendor of Malta. Here's a complete guide to boat trips and cruises:

Blue Lagoon:
A visit to the Blue Lagoon, situated on the small island of Comino, is a must for boat enthusiasts. Take a boat trip from Malta or Gozo to this picturesque paradise, characterized by its turquoise waters and white sandy seabed. Relax on the deck of a boat, swim in the crystal-clear lagoon, and soak up the sun on the pristine beaches.

Comino Caves:

Explore the captivating sea caves that surround the island of Comino. Join a boat tour that takes you along the rugged coastline, allowing you to marvel at the natural formations and shimmering blue waters. Discover hidden caves, arches, and rock formations as you cruise through this scenic area.

Gozo Coastal Cruise:
Embark on a coastal cruise around the sister island of Gozo to experience its beauty from a different perspective. Cruise along the rugged cliffs, pass by charming fishing villages, and admire breathtaking coastal panoramas. Some cruises also include stops for swimming and snorkeling in secluded bays.

Valletta Harbor Cruise:
Discover the grandeur of Valletta, Malta's capital city, with a harbor cruise. Sail along the iconic Grand Harbor, admiring the impressive fortifications, historic buildings, and panoramic views of Valletta's skyline. Learn about the city's rich maritime history and witness the bustling

activity of one of the most picturesque harbors in the Mediterranean.

Sunset Cruises:

Indulge in the romance of a sunset cruise along Malta's coastline. Relax on deck as the sun sets over the horizon, casting a warm glow on the surrounding waters. Enjoy a leisurely sail, sip on a refreshing drink, and embrace the tranquility of the Mediterranean Sea during this magical experience.

Gozo and Comino Excursions:

Combine the best of both worlds with an excursion that includes visits to Gozo and Comino. Explore the highlights of Gozo, such as the Azure Window (until its collapse in 2017), the Citadel, and the island's charming villages. Then, sail to Comino and spend time at the Blue Lagoon, snorkeling in its crystal-clear waters and basking in its natural beauty.

Private Charters:

For a more personalized experience, consider chartering a private boat or yacht. Tailor your itinerary to your preferences, whether it's exploring hidden coves, snorkeling in secluded spots, or simply cruising along the coast at your own pace. Private charters offer exclusivity, comfort, and the freedom to design your ideal maritime adventure.

Diving and Snorkeling Boat Trips:
If you're a diving or snorkeling enthusiast, join a boat trip specifically designed for underwater exploration. Dive into Malta's clear waters and discover vibrant reefs, fascinating caves, and historic shipwrecks. Professional dive guides and instructors will ensure your safety and provide an unforgettable underwater experience.

When participating in boat trips and cruises, remember to follow safety instructions, respect the marine environment, and adhere to local regulations. Choose a reputable operator that prioritizes environmental sustainability and conservation. Enjoy the scenic vistas, the refreshing sea breeze, and the thrill of exploring Malta's coastal wonders from the comfort of a boat.

CYCLING AND SEGWAY TOURS

For those seeking an active and unique way to explore Malta, cycling and Segway tours offer an exciting and convenient way to navigate the island's picturesque landscapes and historic sites. With its diverse terrain and rich cultural heritage, Malta provides a fantastic backdrop for two-wheeled adventures. Here's a complete guide to cycling and Segway tours in Malta:

Valletta City Tour:
Discover the charms of Malta's capital city, Valletta, on a cycling or Segway tour. Navigate the narrow streets and historic squares as you explore this UNESCO World Heritage site. Admire the grand architecture, visit iconic landmarks like St. John's Co-Cathedral, and learn about the city's fascinating history from knowledgeable guides.

Three Cities Tour:

Embark on a cycling or Segway tour of the Three Cities—Vittoriosa, Senglea, and Cospicua. Pedal or glide through narrow alleys, past ancient fortifications, and along the scenic waterfront. Immerse yourself in the historical ambiance of these fortified cities, each with its own unique character and stories to tell.

Dingli Cliffs and Countryside:
Enjoy a cycling tour through the tranquil countryside and along the breathtaking Dingli Cliffs. Pedal along scenic routes, passing through quaint villages and enjoying panoramic views of the Mediterranean Sea. Take in the fresh air and picturesque landscapes as you explore one of Malta's most scenic areas.

Gozo Island Cycling Tour:
Hop on a ferry and embark on a cycling adventure on Gozo, Malta's sister island. Explore the island's charming villages, rolling hills, and idyllic countryside. Cycle past megalithic temples, visit

picturesque coastal towns like Xlendi, and take in the panoramic views from high vantage points. Gozo's smaller size and scenic routes make it a cyclist's paradise.

Marsaxlokk and the South Coast:
Discover the vibrant fishing village of Marsaxlokk and the scenic beauty of Malta's south coast on a cycling or Segway tour. Ride along the coast, passing by colorful fishing boats, quaint harbors, and traditional Maltese houses. Explore hidden coves, take in stunning sea views, and indulge in fresh seafood along the way.

Mdina and Rabat:
Experience the ancient walled city of Mdina and its neighboring town, Rabat, on a cycling or Segway tour. Ride through narrow, winding streets, marvel at medieval architecture, and visit historic sites like St. Paul's Catacombs. Explore the charm and history of these cultural gems at your own pace.

Coastal Bike Trails:

Malta offers a variety of coastal bike trails that allow you to explore the island's stunning shoreline. From St. Julian's to St. Paul's Bay or Mellieħa, these scenic routes offer picturesque views, sea breezes, and opportunities to stop and swim at beautiful beaches along the way. Rent a bike and embark on a coastal adventure.

Segway Tours in Urban Areas:

Segway tours are a fun and efficient way to explore urban areas such as Sliema, St. Julian's, and Bugibba. Glide along the promenades, enjoy panoramic sea views, and explore bustling streets lined with shops, restaurants, and attractions. Segways provide a unique and eco-friendly way to get around and see the sights.

Before embarking on cycling or Segway tours, ensure that you wear appropriate safety gear, follow traffic rules, and adhere to local regulations. Choose reputable tour operators that provide well-maintained equipment, knowledgeable guides, and prioritize safety. Whether you choose to pedal or glide, these tours offer an exhilarating and immersive way to experience the beauty and history of Malta.

CHAPTER 6

MALTESE CUISINE AND DINING

Maltese cuisine is a delightful fusion of Mediterranean flavors, influenced by the island's rich history and cultural diversity. From fresh seafood to hearty stews and savory pastries, Malta offers a variety of culinary delights that will satisfy every palate. In this chapter, we explore the unique dishes, traditional ingredients, and dining experiences that await you in Malta. Get ready to indulge in the flavors of the island.

Traditional Maltese Dishes:

a. Fenkata: A beloved Maltese dish, fenkata is a rabbit stew slow-cooked with garlic, wine, and herbs. It is typically enjoyed as a festive communal meal.

b. Stuffat tal-Fenek: This rabbit stew is another popular Maltese specialty, prepared with tomato sauce, red wine, onions, and aromatic spices.

c. Timpana: A mouthwatering baked pasta dish consisting of macaroni, minced beef, eggs, and a savory tomato sauce.

d. Pastizzi: A must-try Maltese snack, pastizzi are flaky pastry parcels filled with either ricotta cheese (pastizzi tal-irkotta) or mushy peas (pastizzi tal-piżelli).

Fresh Seafood:

Given its island location, Malta boasts an abundance of fresh seafood. Indulge in dishes like lampuki (dolphin fish) pie, calamari (squid), octopus stew, and grilled swordfish. Visit fishing villages such as Marsaxlokk to savor the catch of the day at local waterfront restaurants.

Maltese Bread and Ftira:

Maltese bread, known as "Ħobż tal-Malti," is a staple in the Maltese diet. It has a crusty exterior and a soft, dense interior. Enjoy it with olive oil, dips, or as a base for sandwiches. Another traditional bread is ftira, a round, flatbread topped with various ingredients such as tomatoes, olives, capers, and tuna.

Gozo Cheese:

Gozo, Malta's sister island, is renowned for its delicious cheese. Taste varieties like gbejna, a small cheese made from sheep's or goat's milk, which can be served fresh or dried and flavored with pepper or herbs.

Maltese Sweets and Desserts:

Satisfy your sweet tooth with traditional Maltese desserts. Try the popular Imqaret, deep-fried date pastries sprinkled with powdered sugar. Other treats include kannoli, a tube-shaped pastry filled with sweet ricotta, and helwa tat-tork, a nougat-like sweet made with almonds and honey.

Dining Experiences:

Experience Maltese hospitality by dining at local restaurants, known as "bandli" or "konobas." These establishments offer a cozy atmosphere and serve authentic Maltese dishes. Try "fenkata" nights, where you can enjoy a rabbit feast with live music and entertainment. Don't miss the opportunity to savor a traditional Maltese Sunday lunch, often served in family-run farmhouses.

Wine and Beer:
Malta has a growing wine industry, and its vineyards produce a range of excellent wines. Sample local varietals such as Girgentina and Gellewza, or visit wineries for tastings. Additionally, try Cisk, the popular Maltese beer, and experience the local brewing traditions.

Cultural Festivals and Food Events:
Plan your visit to coincide with culinary events and festivals that celebrate Maltese cuisine. The Malta International Food Festival and the Strawberry Festival are just a few examples of events where you can taste an array of local and international dishes.

Immerse yourself in the flavors of Malta, explore the local markets, and indulge in traditional Maltese dishes. From hearty stews to delectable pastries, the Maltese cuisine will leave you with a lasting impression of the island's gastronomic delights.

TRADITIONAL MALTESE DISHES

Maltese cuisine is a reflection of the island's rich history and cultural influences. From hearty stews to savory pastries and delightful sweets, the traditional dishes of Malta offer a unique blend of Mediterranean flavors. Prepare your taste buds for a gastronomic journey as we explore some of the must-try traditional Maltese dishes:

Fenkata:
Fenkata is a beloved Maltese dish that is deeply rooted in the island's culinary traditions. This hearty rabbit stew is slow-cooked with garlic, wine, herbs, and spices. Fenkata is often enjoyed as a communal meal, bringing family and friends together around the table to savor the tender and flavorful rabbit meat.

Stuffat tal-Fenek:
Another popular rabbit dish in Malta is Stuffat tal-Fenek. This flavorful stew features rabbit pieces

simmered in a rich tomato sauce, red wine, onions, and aromatic herbs. The slow cooking process allows the flavors to meld together, resulting in a deliciously tender and comforting dish.

Timpana:

Timpana is a mouthwatering baked pasta dish that holds a special place in Maltese cuisine. It consists of macaroni mixed with a flavorful tomato sauce, minced beef, eggs, and sometimes peas. The mixture is then baked to perfection, creating a savory and satisfying dish that is a favorite at family gatherings and festive occasions.

Pastizzi:

No visit to Malta is complete without trying pastizzi. These flaky pastry parcels are filled with either ricotta cheese (pastizzi tal-irkotta) or mushy peas (pastizzi tal-piżelli). Pastizzi are a popular snack or breakfast option, enjoyed by locals and visitors alike. Pair them with a cup of tea or coffee for a delightful morning treat.

Bragioli:

Bragioli is a traditional Maltese dish consisting of thin slices of beef rolled around a filling of minced beef, bacon, garlic, and parsley. The rolls are then simmered in a rich tomato-based sauce until tender and flavorful. Bragioli is often served as a main course accompanied by mashed potatoes or pasta.

Kapunata:

Kapunata is Malta's version of ratatouille, a vegetable medley bursting with flavors. It typically includes eggplant, bell peppers, tomatoes, onions, garlic, and various herbs and spices. Kapunata can be enjoyed as a side dish or as a topping for crusty Maltese bread.

Aljotta:

Aljotta is a traditional Maltese fish soup that showcases the island's abundant seafood. It features a flavorful broth made with fish, onions, garlic, tomatoes, herbs, and a splash of lemon juice.

Aljotta is often served with crusty bread, making it a comforting and nourishing dish.

Imqaret:
Imqaret is a delightful sweet treat that you simply can't miss. These deep-fried date pastries are made by wrapping a mixture of dates, orange peel, and spices in a thin pastry dough. The imqaret are then fried until golden and crispy, resulting in a delectable combination of textures and flavors.

These are just a few examples of the traditional Maltese dishes that await you on your culinary journey through Malta. As you explore the island, be sure to savor these authentic flavors and immerse yourself in the rich culinary heritage that Malta has to offer.

LOCAL FOOD MARKETS AND FESTIVALS

To truly experience the vibrant culinary scene of Malta, exploring local food markets and attending food festivals is a must. These lively gatherings offer an opportunity to taste and discover the freshest local produce, traditional delicacies, and diverse flavors that define Maltese cuisine. Here are some renowned food markets and festivals in Malta that will immerse you in the island's gastronomic culture:

Marsaxlokk Fish Market:
Located in the picturesque fishing village of Marsaxlokk, the Marsaxlokk Fish Market is a must-visit for seafood enthusiasts. Every Sunday morning, the harbor comes alive with stalls showcasing an impressive variety of freshly caught fish and shellfish. Immerse yourself in the vibrant atmosphere, interact with local fishermen, and choose your favorite seafood to savor later.

Valletta Market:

The Valletta Market, also known as the Is-Suq Tal-Belt, is a bustling food market located in Malta's capital city. Housed in a beautifully restored building, this market offers a delightful array of local and international produce, gourmet treats, and traditional Maltese products. From fresh fruits and vegetables to artisanal cheeses, olives, pastries, and wines, you'll find a treasure trove of flavors to explore.

The Chocolate Festival:

Indulge your sweet tooth at The Chocolate Festival held in Ħamrun, a town in central Malta. This annual festival celebrates all things chocolate, showcasing a wide range of delectable treats from local and international chocolatiers. From artisanal chocolates to chocolate desserts and hot cocoa, this event is a paradise for chocolate lovers.

Strawberry Festival:

If you happen to visit Malta in spring, don't miss the Strawberry Festival in the village of Mġarr. This festive event pays homage to the luscious strawberries grown locally. Enjoy a variety of strawberry-based products, including desserts, preserves, and refreshing drinks. The festival features live music, entertainment, and a jovial atmosphere for all to enjoy.

Delicata Wine Festival:

For wine enthusiasts, the Delicata Wine Festival is a must-attend event. Held annually at the Upper Barrakka Gardens in Valletta, this festival showcases a wide selection of local wines produced by Delicata Winery. Sample different varietals, learn about the winemaking process, and indulge in the harmonious flavors of Maltese wine accompanied by live music and entertainment.

Mdina Medieval Festival:

The Mdina Medieval Festival is a captivating event that takes visitors back in time to experience the enchantment of the Middle Ages. While the festival offers much more than just food, it features traditional food stalls offering medieval-inspired dishes. Feast on roasted meats, hearty stews, and other rustic fare while enjoying live performances, reenactments, and a lively medieval atmosphere.

Malta International Food Festival:

The Malta International Food Festival is a celebration of global cuisine, bringing together flavors from around the world in one place. Held in Valletta, this annual event showcases an impressive range of international dishes prepared by local and foreign chefs. From Asian street food to Mediterranean specialties and everything in between, the festival offers a culinary journey for visitors to savor.

Gozo Food and Wine Festival:

If you're visiting Gozo, Malta's sister island, don't miss the Gozo Food and Wine Festival. Held in the charming village of Xewkija, this event highlights

Gozitan produce, traditional dishes, and local wines. Sample artisanal cheeses, olive oils, Gozitan delicacies, and sip on wines while enjoying live music and cultural performances.

These food markets and festivals provide a fantastic opportunity to engage with the local culinary scene, taste authentic flavors, and discover the diverse and rich food heritage of Malta. Plan your visit accordingly to immerse yourself in these vibrant celebrations of food and culture.

POPULAR RESTAURANTS AND CAFÉS

Malta is home to a thriving culinary scene with a wide range of restaurants and cafés that cater to various tastes and preferences. From traditional Maltese dishes to international cuisine, these establishments offer a delectable dining experience that will satisfy even the most discerning palate. Here are some popular restaurants and cafés in Malta that you should consider visiting:

Rampila Restaurant (Valletta):
Situated within the historic ramparts of Valletta, Rampila Restaurant offers a unique dining experience in a charming setting. Enjoy a blend of Maltese and Mediterranean cuisine while surrounded by the atmospheric ambiance of the ancient fortress walls.

Ta' Marija (Mġarr):
Ta' Marija is a renowned Maltese restaurant located in the village of Mġarr. It is famous for its authentic

Maltese dishes, live folk music, and traditional entertainment. Indulge in local specialties like rabbit stew and enjoy a vibrant cultural experience.

Legligin Wine Bar (Valletta):
For wine enthusiasts, Legligin Wine Bar in Valletta is a must-visit. This cozy bar offers an extensive selection of local and international wines, accompanied by a variety of delicious tapas-style dishes. Relax in the intimate atmosphere and savor the flavors of carefully curated wine and food pairings.

Noni (Valletta):
Noni is a contemporary restaurant located in Valletta, known for its innovative approach to Maltese cuisine. Led by Chef Jonathan Brincat, Noni offers a refined dining experience with a menu that showcases the finest local ingredients transformed into creative and flavorful dishes.

Ta' Kris (Sliema):

Ta' Kris is a charming restaurant nestled in the heart of Sliema. It is celebrated for its authentic Maltese cuisine, including dishes like rabbit, bragioli, and fenkata. With its cozy atmosphere and friendly service, Ta' Kris provides a delightful taste of traditional Maltese flavors.

The Harbour Club (Valletta):
Overlooking the Grand Harbour in Valletta, The Harbour Club offers a luxurious dining experience. With a focus on fresh seafood and Mediterranean cuisine, this restaurant serves beautifully presented dishes in a stunning waterfront setting.

Fontanella Tea Garden (Mdina):
Fontanella Tea Garden is a renowned café located within the ancient walls of Mdina, the historic fortified city. Famous for its decadent cakes and pastries, this café is the perfect spot to relax and enjoy stunning views while indulging in a sweet treat.

Mint (Sliema):

Mint is a trendy café and restaurant located in Sliema, offering a diverse menu inspired by Mediterranean and Asian flavors. From gourmet burgers to sushi, Mint caters to a wide range of tastes and provides a vibrant and contemporary dining experience.

Ta' Frenc (Gozo):

For those exploring Gozo, Ta' Frenc is a must-visit restaurant. Located in a charming farmhouse, it offers a refined dining experience with a menu that highlights local produce and flavors. Ta' Frenc is known for its warm hospitality and exquisite dishes crafted with creativity and precision.

Busy Bee Café (Marsaxlokk):

If you're looking for a casual dining experience with a focus on fresh seafood, Busy Bee Café in Marsaxlokk is a popular choice. Sample the catch of the day while enjoying the relaxed atmosphere of this charming seaside café.

These are just a few examples of the many exceptional restaurants and cafés that await you in Malta. Whether you're seeking traditional Maltese flavors or international cuisine, these establishments promise a memorable dining experience that will leave you craving for more.

WINE AND BEER TASTING

Malta is not only known for its rich history and stunning landscapes but also for its vibrant wine and beer culture. Whether you're a wine connoisseur or a beer enthusiast, the island offers plenty of opportunities to indulge in tastings and explore the unique flavors of locally produced beverages. Here are some experiences you shouldn't miss when it comes to wine and beer tasting in Malta:

Wine Tasting:

Marsovin Wine Cellars (Marsa):
Marsovin is one of Malta's most renowned wineries, and a visit to their wine cellars in Marsa is a must for wine lovers. Take a guided tour to learn about the winemaking process, explore the aging cellars, and, most importantly, savor a variety of their award-winning wines through a guided tasting.

Delicata Winery (Paola):

Delicata Winery is another prominent name in Maltese winemaking. Visit their estate in Paola for a fascinating tour that takes you through their vineyards and cellars. The experience culminates with a wine tasting, where you can sample a selection of their wines, including the popular Medina range.

Meridiana Wine Estate (Ta' Qali):

Located in the picturesque Ta' Qali countryside, Meridiana Wine Estate offers visitors a chance to immerse themselves in the world of Maltese wine. Join a guided tour to discover their vineyards and winemaking facilities, followed by a wine tasting session where you can appreciate the unique flavors of their estate-grown wines.

Wine Bars and Restaurants:

Throughout Malta, you'll find wine bars and restaurants that offer extensive wine lists showcasing both local and international selections.

Visit places like Trabuxu Wine Bar in Valletta or Ta' Philip Restaurant in Marsaxlokk, where you can savor a wide range of wines while enjoying delicious food pairings.

Beer Tasting:

Lord Chambray Brewery (Gozo):
Lord Chambray Brewery, located in the picturesque village of Xewkija in Gozo, is the first craft brewery in Malta. Take a guided tour of their facilities to learn about their brewing techniques and ingredients. Afterward, enjoy a beer tasting session to sample their range of craft beers, including pale ales, IPAs, and lagers.

The Beer Cave (Valletta):
Nestled within the historic walls of Valletta, The Beer Cave is a popular destination for beer enthusiasts. This cozy bar boasts an extensive selection of local and international craft beers. Explore their wide range of styles and flavors, and

let the knowledgeable staff guide you through a memorable beer tasting experience.

BrewHaus (Sliema):

BrewHaus is a lively beer bar located in Sliema, offering an impressive selection of craft beers from around the world. With a rotating tap list and an extensive bottle collection, you'll have the opportunity to sample a diverse range of flavors and styles while enjoying the vibrant atmosphere.

Beer Festivals:

Keep an eye out for beer festivals that take place in Malta throughout the year. These events bring together local and international breweries, offering a great opportunity to sample a wide variety of beers. The Craft Beer Festival and Oktoberfest Malta are two notable festivals that celebrate the beer culture on the island.

Whether you prefer wine or beer, the wine cellars, bars, and festivals of Malta provide a delightful journey into the flavors and craftsmanship of locally produced beverages. Raise a glass, savor the unique tastes, and toast to the rich brewing and winemaking traditions of the island.

CHAPTER 7
CULTURAL EXPERIENCES IN MALTA

Malta is a treasure trove of cultural experiences, offering a blend of ancient traditions, historical landmarks, and vibrant festivals. Immerse yourself in the island's rich heritage by exploring its cultural attractions and participating in unique events. Here are some noteworthy cultural experiences to add to your itinerary:

Heritage Sites and Museums:
Discover Malta's fascinating history by visiting its heritage sites and museums. Explore the UNESCO World Heritage Sites of Ħal Saflieni Hypogeum, a subterranean necropolis, and the megalithic temples of Ġgantija. Don't miss the National Museum of Archaeology and the National Museum of Fine Arts in Valletta, which provide a comprehensive insight into the island's art and archaeology.

The Malta International Arts Festival:

If you visit Malta during the summer months, the Malta International Arts Festival is a must-attend event. This multidisciplinary festival showcases a diverse range of performances, including music, theater, dance, and visual arts. Experience world-class productions and engage with artists from around the globe.

Carnival:

Experience the vibrant spirit of Malta by joining in the Carnival festivities. Held in February, Carnival is a lively celebration characterized by colorful parades, extravagant costumes, music, and dancing. The main Carnival events take place in Valletta and the village of Nadur in Gozo, offering a unique glimpse into Maltese traditions and folklore.

Religious Celebrations:

Malta is deeply rooted in religious traditions, and attending religious celebrations provides a window into the local culture. Witness the grandeur of religious processions, such as the Good Friday processions in various towns, or the festa celebrations dedicated to patron saints in different villages throughout the year. These events showcase elaborate decorations, fireworks, marching bands, and religious rituals.

Maltese Folklore and Crafts:
Immerse yourself in the rich folklore and traditional crafts of Malta. Visit the Ta' Qali Crafts Village, where you can observe artisans creating intricate lace, pottery, and filigree jewelry. Explore the streets of villages like Qormi and Żebbuġ, known for their traditional festoons and decorative street displays during local celebrations.

Maltese Cuisine Workshops:
Delve into the flavors of Maltese cuisine by participating in cooking workshops and culinary experiences. Learn to prepare traditional dishes like rabbit stew, pastizzi (flaky pastries filled with ricotta or mushy peas), and ftira (Maltese bread)

under the guidance of local chefs. Discover the secrets of Maltese flavors and bring a taste of Malta back home with you.

The Mdina Medieval Festival:
Step back in time during the Mdina Medieval Festival, a spectacular event that recreates the medieval era in the ancient fortified city of Mdina. Witness jousting tournaments, falconry displays, reenactments, and costumed performances. This immersive experience allows you to feel as though you've stepped into a medieval world.

Language and Cultural Exchange:
Engage with the locals and deepen your understanding of Maltese culture through language and cultural exchange programs. Join language courses to learn the Maltese language or participate in cultural workshops where you can learn traditional Maltese dances, music, and crafts. This hands-on experience will give you a deeper appreciation of the local culture.

Traditional Music and Dance:

Attend performances of traditional Maltese music and dance to witness the island's vibrant cultural heritage. The Maltese għana (folk singing) and the Maltese band clubs that perform during festa celebrations are particularly noteworthy. Experience the rhythmic beats, lively melodies, and passionate performances that bring the traditions to life.

Street Markets and Artisan Fairs:

Explore the local street markets and artisan fairs that showcase Maltese craftsmanship and local products. The Marsaxlokk Fish Market, held on Sundays, is a bustling market where you can find fresh seafood and local delicacies. Additionally, various artisan fairs are organized throughout the year, providing an opportunity to purchase unique handmade crafts and artworks.

By immersing yourself in these cultural experiences, you'll gain a deeper appreciation for Malta's history, traditions, and artistic expressions. Embrace the island's vibrant cultural scene and create lasting memories of your visit.

FESTIVALS AND EVENTS

Malta is known for its lively and vibrant festivals and events, which showcase the island's rich cultural heritage, religious traditions, music, arts, and more. Immerse yourself in the festive atmosphere and join the locals in celebrating these exciting occasions. Here are some of the most popular festivals and events in Malta:

Malta International Fireworks Festival:
Experience a spectacle of light and sound at the Malta International Fireworks Festival. Held annually in April, this event brings together pyrotechnic teams from around the world to compete and showcase their skills. Enjoy breathtaking fireworks displays set against the backdrop of Malta's stunning skyline.

Isle of MTV Malta:
If you're a music lover, don't miss the Isle of MTV Malta festival. This free open-air music event takes

place in July and features performances by internationally renowned artists and DJs. Join thousands of music enthusiasts and dance the night away in the heart of Malta.

Valletta International Baroque Festival:
The Valletta International Baroque Festival is a celebration of Baroque music, art, and culture. Held in January, this festival features concerts, recitals, and performances by world-class musicians in historic venues across Valletta. Immerse yourself in the grandeur of Baroque music during this cultural extravaganza.

Malta Arts Festival:
The Malta Arts Festival is a multidisciplinary arts festival held in July and August. It showcases a diverse range of performances, including music, dance, theater, visual arts, and more. Explore the vibrant artistic expressions of local and international artists in various locations across Malta.

BirguFest:

BirguFest, also known as Birgu by Candlelight, is a unique event held in October in the fortified city of Birgu (Vittoriosa). The city is lit solely by candles, creating a magical ambiance. Visitors can enjoy live music, historical reenactments, food stalls, and guided tours of the city's historical sites.

Carnival:

Carnival is a highly anticipated event in Malta, celebrated with great enthusiasm and color. Join in the festivities in February, when the streets come alive with parades, elaborate floats, and vibrant costumes. Experience the joyous atmosphere, music, and dancing as locals and visitors revel in the spirit of Carnival.

International Jazz Festival:

Music enthusiasts should not miss the International Jazz Festival, held in July. This prestigious event attracts renowned jazz musicians from around the world, who perform in stunning outdoor venues. Immerse yourself in the smooth melodies and improvisations of jazz in the beautiful setting of Malta.

Feast of Santa Marija:

The Feast of Santa Marija, celebrated on August 15th, is one of the largest religious feasts in Malta. The festa, or village feast, takes place in various towns and villages across the island. Witness colorful processions, traditional band marches, elaborate decorations, and spectacular fireworks as the locals honor the Assumption of the Virgin Mary.

Notte Bianca:

Notte Bianca, meaning "White Night," is a cultural event held in Valletta in October. The city comes alive with a nocturnal celebration of arts and culture. Enjoy exhibitions, live performances, street art, open-air concerts, and various activities that transform Valletta into a bustling hub of creativity.

Christmas and New Year Celebrations:

Experience the festive season in Malta with a range of Christmas and New Year celebrations. Explore the beautifully decorated streets, attend Christmas markets, and enjoy traditional carol singing. Join in the countdown to the New Year with fireworks displays and lively parties across the island.

These festivals and events highlight the cultural diversity and vibrant spirit of Malta. Plan your visit accordingly to immerse yourself in the excitement and celebration that these occasions offer. Celebrate with the locals, enjoy the performances, and create unforgettable memories of your time in Malta.

MUSEUMS AND ART GALLERIES

Malta is home to a wealth of museums and art galleries that provide insight into its rich history, archaeology, art, and culture. From ancient artifacts to contemporary artworks, these institutions offer a fascinating journey through the island's heritage. Here are some prominent museums and art galleries you should consider visiting during your stay in Malta:

The National Museum of Archaeology (Valletta):
Located in Valletta, the National Museum of Archaeology houses an exceptional collection of prehistoric artifacts, including the iconic Venus of Malta and the impressive Ġgantija temple figurines. Explore the island's ancient past and learn about its megalithic temples, burial sites, and other archaeological treasures.

The Palace State Rooms and Armoury (Valletta):

Within the Grandmaster's Palace in Valletta, the Palace State Rooms and Armoury offer a glimpse into Malta's rich history and the grandeur of the Knights of St. John. Marvel at the opulent interiors, historical artifacts, and an extensive collection of weaponry and armor.

The National War Museum (Valletta):
Housed in the historic Fort St. Elmo in Valletta, the National War Museum presents Malta's military history and its role during World War I and World War II. Discover wartime artifacts, personal stories, and interactive displays that provide an immersive understanding of Malta's war experiences.

MUŻA - The Malta National Community Art Museum (Valletta):
MUŻA, located in the Auberge d'Italie in Valletta, is Malta's flagship art museum. It showcases a diverse collection of artworks, including paintings, sculptures, and decorative arts from various periods. Experience the vibrant Maltese art scene

and explore the cultural identity through contemporary and traditional works.

The Malta Maritime Museum (Birgu):
Situated in the former Royal Naval Bakery in Birgu (Vittoriosa), the Malta Maritime Museum celebrates the island's maritime heritage. Discover the maritime history of Malta through exhibits that include model ships, navigation instruments, weaponry, and interactive displays.

The Mdina Experience (Mdina):
Take a journey through the history of the ancient city of Mdina at The Mdina Experience. This multimedia attraction presents the story of Mdina, capturing its unique atmosphere, architecture, and historical significance. Gain a deeper understanding of this enchanting city and its cultural heritage.

The Malta Classic Car Museum (Qawra):
For automobile enthusiasts, the Malta Classic Car Museum in Qawra is a must-visit. It houses a

remarkable collection of vintage and classic cars, showcasing automotive history and craftsmanship. Admire beautifully restored vehicles from different eras and learn about their significance.

The St. John's Co-Cathedral and Museum (Valletta):
Apart from its religious significance, St. John's Co-Cathedral in Valletta houses a museum that displays a stunning collection of religious art and artifacts. Marvel at the intricate Caravaggio paintings, tapestries, silverware, and illuminated manuscripts, all showcasing the grandeur of the Knights of St. John.

The Contemporary Art Space of St. James Cavalier (Valletta):
Situated in Valletta's historic St. James Cavalier building, the Contemporary Art Space hosts a dynamic program of contemporary art exhibitions, performances, and cultural events. Experience the contemporary art scene in Malta and engage with

thought-provoking artworks across various mediums.

The Malta Aviation Museum (Ta' Qali):
Aviation enthusiasts will appreciate the Malta Aviation Museum, located in Ta' Qali. Discover the fascinating history of aviation in Malta through vintage aircraft displays, aviation artifacts, and engaging exhibitions that chronicle Malta's aviation heritage.

These museums and art galleries provide a comprehensive understanding of Malta's history, art, and cultural identity. Take the time to explore them and delve into the captivating stories and artistic expressions that shape the island's heritage.

MALTESE FOLKLORE AND TRADITIONS

Malta is steeped in folklore and traditions that have been passed down through generations, reflecting the island's rich cultural heritage. From colorful festivals to age-old customs, these cultural practices provide a window into Malta's unique identity. Here are some notable Maltese folklore and traditions that you can explore:

Village Festas:
Village festas are an integral part of Maltese culture and take place throughout the year in various towns and villages. These religious feasts celebrate the patron saints of each locality and involve processions, band marches, fireworks, and elaborate decorations. Experience the vibrant atmosphere, join in the festivities, and witness the deep devotion of the locals.

Għana (Maltese Folk Singing):

Għana is a traditional form of Maltese folk singing characterized by improvised lyrics and a distinctive rhythm. These heartfelt songs often convey stories of love, historical events, or social commentary. Attend a Għana session or festival to appreciate this unique musical tradition and connect with the soul of the Maltese people.

Carnival Celebrations:
Carnival is a highly anticipated event in Malta, celebrated with great enthusiasm and creativity. The festivities involve colorful parades, masked revelers, and elaborate costumes. Immerse yourself in the carnival spirit, join in the revelry, and witness the joyous atmosphere that fills the streets during this time.

Traditional Crafts:
Malta boasts a rich tradition of craftsmanship, with artisans practicing traditional skills that have been passed down through generations. Visit local artisans and workshops to witness the creation of

intricate lacework (bizzilla), silver filigree (għanjus), pottery, and basket weaving. These crafts serve as a testament to the island's cultural heritage.

Traditional Maltese Weddings:
Traditional Maltese weddings are full of customs and rituals that have been practiced for centuries. From the procession through the streets to the traditional feasts, these weddings provide a glimpse into the island's traditional social fabric. Experience the joyous celebrations, taste traditional wedding sweets, and witness the unique customs associated with this special occasion.

Fishing Traditions:
Malta's history and culture have deep ties to the sea, and fishing has played a significant role in the island's livelihood. Explore fishing villages such as Marsaxlokk and witness the traditional luzzu boats, adorned with colorful eyes for protection. Engage

with local fishermen, learn about their craft, and savor freshly caught seafood from the local markets.

Holy Week and Easter Traditions:
Holy Week and Easter are marked by a series of religious processions and traditions. Attend the solemn Good Friday processions, where statues depicting biblical scenes are carried through the streets. Witness the spectacle of the Resurrection Sunday morning procession, celebrating the joyous resurrection of Christ.

Festa tal-Ġimgħa l-Kbira (Feast of the Assumption):
The Feast of the Assumption on August 15th is one of the largest religious feasts in Malta. The highlight of this festa is the procession carrying the statue of the Assumption of the Virgin Mary through the streets. Experience the religious fervor, admire the ornate decorations, and participate in the vibrant celebrations.

Traditional Maltese Cuisine:

Maltese cuisine is deeply rooted in local traditions and reflects the island's history and influences from various cultures. Indulge in traditional dishes such as rabbit stew (fenek), pastizzi (savory pastries), and ftira (Maltese bread). Explore the unique flavors and culinary heritage that make Maltese cuisine special.

Folklore and Superstitions:

Malta has its share of folklore, legends, and superstitions that have been passed down through generations. From tales of mystical creatures like the Kaw Kaw to beliefs in the power of amulets and talismans, these traditions offer a glimpse into the island's folklore and cultural beliefs.

Immersing yourself in Maltese folklore and traditions provides a deeper understanding of the island's cultural fabric and offers a chance to connect with its vibrant heritage. Embrace the customs, engage with the locals, and create lasting memories of these unique cultural experiences.

THE KNIGHTS OF MALTA

The Knights of Malta, officially known as the Sovereign Military Hospitaller Order of Saint John of Jerusalem, of Rhodes, and of Malta, have played a significant role in Malta's history and have left an indelible mark on the island. Here is a comprehensive overview of the Knights of Malta and their legacy in Malta:

Origins and Purpose:
The Order of the Knights of Malta was founded in the 11th century as a religious order dedicated to providing medical care and assistance to pilgrims in Jerusalem. Following the loss of the Holy Land, the Knights relocated to Rhodes in the 14th century and later settled in Malta in 1530, where they established their headquarters.

The Great Siege of Malta:
One of the most notable events in the history of the Knights of Malta is the Great Siege of Malta in 1565.

The Ottoman Empire launched a massive invasion, seeking to capture the island. The Knights, under the leadership of Grand Master Jean Parisot de Valette, successfully defended Malta against overwhelming odds, securing their place in history.

Fortifications and Valletta:

As a result of the Great Siege, the Knights realized the need for stronger fortifications to protect the island. They embarked on an ambitious project to build a fortified city, resulting in the creation of Valletta, named after Grand Master Valette. Valletta, with its impressive bastions and fortifications, stands as a testament to the military prowess of the Knights.

Contributions to Art and Architecture:

The Knights of Malta had a significant influence on the artistic and architectural landscape of Malta. They commissioned and sponsored the construction of magnificent palaces, churches, and other structures, many of which still stand today.

The Co-Cathedral of St. John in Valletta, renowned for its opulent interior and Caravaggio paintings, is a prime example of their patronage.

Hospitaller Order and Charity:
The Knights of Malta maintained their original purpose as a hospitaller order, providing medical care and assistance to the sick and the needy. They operated hospitals, infirmaries, and pharmacies, serving not only the Knights themselves but also the local population. The legacy of their charitable work can still be seen in institutions such as the Sacra Infermeria, which now houses the Mediterranean Conference Centre.

The Loss of Malta:
In 1798, Napoleon Bonaparte launched an invasion of Malta, and the Knights were forced to surrender the island. This marked the end of their rule in Malta, and they eventually settled in Rome, where they continue their work as a sovereign entity.

However, their impact on Malta's history and culture remains deeply ingrained.

Modern-day Influence:
The Knights of Malta maintain a presence in Malta and continue to contribute to various charitable and humanitarian causes. They are involved in healthcare initiatives, social welfare programs, and cultural preservation efforts. Their presence serves as a reminder of their enduring legacy and commitment to the betterment of society.

The Knights of Malta have left an indelible imprint on the history, culture, and architecture of Malta. Their contributions to the island's defense, art, healthcare, and charitable endeavors have shaped its identity and continue to be celebrated. Explore the historical sites, museums, and artifacts associated with the Knights to gain a deeper appreciation for their role in Malta's heritage.

CHAPTER 8
PRACTICAL INFORMATION FOR
TRAVELERS

As you plan your trip to Malta, it's essential to have practical information that will help you navigate the island with ease. This chapter provides you with important details and tips to ensure a smooth and enjoyable travel experience.

Time Zone:

Malta operates on Central European Time (CET), which is UTC+1 during standard time and UTC+2 during daylight saving time.

Electricity:

The standard voltage in Malta is 230V, and the frequency is 50Hz. The power outlets are of the Type G three-pin plug, so make sure to bring the appropriate adapter if needed.

Internet and Communication:

Mobile networks are widely available in Malta, offering reliable coverage across the island. You can easily purchase prepaid SIM cards from various providers to stay connected during your trip. Many hotels, restaurants, and cafes also offer free Wi-Fi for their customers.

Emergency Services:
In case of emergencies, dial 112 to reach the police, ambulance, or fire services. The emergency services in Malta are well-equipped and responsive.

Health and Safety:
Malta has a high standard of healthcare, with both public and private hospitals available. It is advisable to have travel insurance that covers medical expenses during your stay. Additionally, it is recommended to follow standard safety precautions, such as practicing good hygiene and being cautious with your belongings, to ensure a safe trip.

Currency and Money Matters:

The currency in Malta is the Euro (EUR). Credit cards are widely accepted in hotels, restaurants, and larger establishments. ATMs can be found throughout the island, allowing you to withdraw cash in the local currency. It's a good idea to inform your bank of your travel plans to avoid any issues with card usage.

Tipping:

Tipping in Malta is generally discretionary. It is common to leave a 10% tip at restaurants if the service charge is not included. For other services, such as taxi rides or hotel staff, rounding up the bill or offering a small tip is appreciated but not obligatory.

Public Transportation:

Malta has a reliable public transportation system, including buses and ferries, that connect different parts of the island. The public bus service is an affordable and convenient way to travel, with frequent routes and schedules. You can also hire taxis or rent a car for more flexibility in exploring the island.

Language:
The official languages of Malta are Maltese and English. English is widely spoken and understood, making communication easy for English-speaking travelers.

Customs and Etiquette:
Respect for local customs and traditions is important when visiting Malta. It is customary to greet people with a handshake and maintain eye contact during conversations. Modest dress is appreciated when visiting religious sites, and it is polite to ask for permission before taking photographs of locals.

Shopping and Business Hours:
Most shops and businesses in Malta operate from Monday to Saturday, with shorter hours on

Saturdays. Larger shopping centers and supermarkets may have extended hours. On Sundays and public holidays, smaller shops may be closed or have limited hours, but some tourist areas and restaurants remain open.

By familiarizing yourself with this practical information, you'll be well-prepared to navigate Malta, respect local customs, and have a hassle-free experience during your visit. Enjoy your time exploring this beautiful Mediterranean destination!

ACCOMMODATION OPTIONS

When planning your trip to Malta, choosing the right accommodation is crucial for a comfortable and enjoyable stay. The island offers a wide range of options to suit different preferences and budgets. Here are some popular accommodation options in Malta:

Hotels and Resorts:
Malta boasts a variety of hotels and resorts, ranging from budget-friendly options to luxurious five-star properties. These establishments offer a host of amenities, including swimming pools, on-site restaurants, spa facilities, and organized activities. Choose a hotel or resort based on your desired location, budget, and preferred level of comfort.

Boutique Hotels:
For a more personalized and intimate experience, consider staying at one of Malta's boutique hotels. These smaller, independently-run accommodations

often offer unique themes, stylish decor, and personalized services. Boutique hotels provide a charming and cozy atmosphere that is perfect for those seeking a more intimate setting.

Guesthouses and Bed & Breakfasts:
Guesthouses and bed & breakfasts are a great option for travelers looking for a homely atmosphere and a chance to interact with the locals. These accommodations offer comfortable rooms and a breakfast service, often prepared with local specialties. Guesthouses are typically family-run and provide a warm and welcoming experience.

Self-Catering Apartments and Villas:
If you prefer more flexibility and independence during your stay, consider renting a self-catering apartment or villa. These options are ideal for families or larger groups, as they provide more space and the convenience of a fully equipped kitchen. Self-catering accommodations allow you to

experience Malta like a local, shopping for fresh ingredients and preparing your meals.

Farmhouses:

In the rural areas of Malta, you can find traditional farmhouses available for rent. These charming properties offer a rustic and authentic experience, with features like stone walls, courtyards, and traditional furnishings. Farmhouses are perfect for those seeking a peaceful retreat and a closer connection to the island's rural lifestyle.

Hostels:

For budget-conscious travelers and solo adventurers, hostels are a popular option. Malta has several hostels that offer dormitory-style rooms and shared facilities, making it a cost-effective choice for accommodation. Hostels often have communal areas where you can socialize with fellow travelers, making it a great option for meeting new people.

Camping and Glamping:

If you enjoy outdoor adventures, Malta has camping sites that allow you to connect with nature. Camping facilities provide basic amenities such as shower blocks, electricity, and designated camping spots. For a more luxurious camping experience, you can also find glamping sites that offer comfortable tents with added amenities and facilities.

Regardless of your preferred accommodation type, it is advisable to book in advance, especially during peak travel seasons, to secure your desired choice. Take into account factors such as location, proximity to attractions, and access to public transportation when making your decision.

Whether you opt for a luxurious hotel, a cozy guesthouse, or a unique farmhouse, finding the right accommodation in Malta will enhance your overall travel experience. Choose a place that suits your needs and preferences, and enjoy your stay on this beautiful Mediterranean island.

HEALTH AND SAFETY TIPS

When traveling to Malta, it's important to prioritize your health and safety to ensure a smooth and enjoyable trip. Here are some essential tips to keep in mind:

Travel Insurance:
Before your trip, make sure you have comprehensive travel insurance that covers medical expenses, trip cancellation or interruption, and personal liability. Check the policy details to understand what is covered and keep a copy of your insurance information handy.

Medical Preparations:
Ensure that you are up to date with routine vaccinations and consider additional vaccinations recommended for Malta. It's also a good idea to pack a basic first aid kit with essential supplies such as bandages, antiseptic cream, pain relievers, and any necessary prescription medications.

Hygiene Precautions:

Maintain good hygiene practices during your trip. Wash your hands frequently with soap and water or use hand sanitizer when handwashing facilities are not available. Avoid touching your face, especially your eyes, nose, and mouth, to minimize the risk of infection.

Sun Protection:

Malta enjoys a sunny Mediterranean climate, so it's essential to protect yourself from the sun. Wear sunscreen with a high SPF, sunglasses, and a wide-brimmed hat to shield yourself from harmful UV rays. Seek shade during the peak hours of sun intensity, usually between 10 am and 4 pm.

Stay Hydrated:

In Malta's warm climate, it's crucial to stay hydrated, especially when spending time outdoors. Carry a water bottle with you and drink plenty of fluids throughout the day. Remember to drink clean, bottled water and avoid consuming tap water unless it has been declared safe for drinking.

Safety Precautions:
Exercise caution and common sense to ensure your personal safety. Be aware of your surroundings, especially in crowded areas and tourist spots. Keep your belongings secure and be vigilant against pickpockets. If you plan to engage in outdoor activities, follow safety guidelines and use proper equipment.

Weather Conditions:
Stay informed about weather conditions, particularly if you are planning outdoor activities or water sports. Malta can experience strong winds and rough seas at times, so it's important to heed warnings and take necessary precautions. Check local weather forecasts and advisories before heading out.

Respect Local Customs:

Respect the local customs and traditions of Malta. Dress appropriately, especially when visiting religious sites. Follow any guidelines or rules in cultural or heritage sites you visit. Be mindful of local sensitivities and act respectfully towards the local population.

Emergency Contacts:

Save important emergency contacts in your phone or keep them easily accessible. This includes the local police (112), ambulance services, and the contact information for your country's embassy or consulate in Malta.

COVID-19 Considerations:

As of the knowledge cutoff in September 2021, COVID-19 measures and guidelines may still be in place. Stay updated on the latest travel advisories, entry requirements, and health protocols related to COVID-19. Follow local guidelines regarding face masks, social distancing, and other precautionary measures.

By following these health and safety tips, you can have a worry-free and enjoyable trip to Malta. Remember to plan ahead, stay informed, and prioritize your well-being throughout your journey.

CUSTOMS AND ETIQUETTE

When visiting Malta, it's important to familiarize yourself with the local customs and etiquette to show respect for the culture and make a positive impression. Here are some customs and etiquette tips to keep in mind during your stay:

Greetings and Politeness:
When meeting someone for the first time or entering a shop or establishment, it's customary to greet people with a handshake and maintain eye contact. Use polite phrases such as "bonġu" (good day) or "lejl it-tajjeb" (good evening) when interacting with locals. It's also polite to say "jekk jogħġbok" (please) and "grazzi" (thank you) in your conversations.

Modest Dress:
When visiting religious sites or attending formal occasions, it's appropriate to dress modestly. Women should cover their shoulders and avoid

wearing revealing clothing. Similarly, men should dress appropriately, avoiding beachwear or overly casual attire in certain settings.

Photography Etiquette:
Before taking photographs of locals or inside religious sites, always seek permission out of respect for privacy and cultural sensitivities. Some areas may have restrictions on photography, so be mindful of any signage or instructions provided.

Language:
The official languages of Malta are Maltese and English. English is widely spoken and understood, so communication should not pose a significant barrier for English-speaking travelers. However, it is appreciated when visitors make an effort to learn a few basic phrases in Maltese, such as greetings and thank you.

Punctuality:

Maltese people generally appreciate punctuality, so it's considered polite to arrive on time for appointments, meetings, or scheduled activities. Being punctual demonstrates respect for others' time and is a common courtesy.

Public Behavior:
When in public spaces, maintain a respectful and considerate demeanor. Avoid littering and keep public areas clean. It's also important to be mindful of noise levels, especially in residential areas, to avoid disturbing the peace and tranquility of the surroundings.

Dining Etiquette:
If invited to someone's home for a meal, it is customary to bring a small gift, such as a bottle of wine or chocolates, as a token of appreciation. During meals, wait until the host or hostess invites you to start eating and use utensils appropriately. Finish your plate as it is a sign of appreciation for the meal.

Tipping:

Tipping in Malta is generally discretionary but appreciated for good service. In restaurants, if the service charge is not included, leaving a 10% tip is customary. For other services such as taxis or hotel staff, rounding up the bill or offering a small tip is considered polite.

Festivals and Traditions:

Malta has a rich cultural calendar, with various festivals and traditions celebrated throughout the year. Respect local customs and traditions by observing and participating with enthusiasm, if appropriate. Learn about the significance of these events and be mindful of any rules or regulations associated with them.

Religious Sensitivities:

Malta is a predominantly Roman Catholic country, and religious customs hold significance. When visiting churches or religious sites, dress modestly and behave respectfully. Avoid loud conversations or disruptive behavior that may disturb those who are praying or attending religious services.

By following these customs and etiquette tips, you'll show respect for the local culture, enhance your interactions with the Maltese people, and have a more immersive and enjoyable experience during your visit to Malta.

EMERGENCY CONTACTS

During your visit to Malta, it's crucial to know the emergency contact numbers to reach out to in case of any urgent situations. Here are the essential emergency contacts you should have readily available:

General Emergency Helpline: 112
The general emergency helpline in Malta is 112. This number connects you to the emergency services, including the police, ambulance, and fire department. It should be used in situations where immediate assistance is required, such as accidents, crimes, or medical emergencies.

Police: 112
If you need to report a crime, seek police assistance, or require any other police-related help, dial 112. The police in Malta are responsible for maintaining law and order, ensuring public safety, and responding to emergency situations.

Ambulance and Medical Emergencies: 112

In case of a medical emergency, such as a severe illness, injury, or any situation requiring urgent medical attention, dial 112. This will connect you to the ambulance services, and trained medical professionals will provide assistance and transport you to the nearest medical facility.

Fire and Rescue Services: 112

If you encounter a fire, a hazardous situation, or require rescue services, dial 112. This will connect you to the fire and rescue services in Malta, who are trained to handle emergencies and provide prompt assistance.

Tourist Helpline: +356 2291 5000

For non-emergency assistance and information specifically for tourists, you can contact the tourist helpline. The number for the tourist helpline in Malta is +356 2291 5000. They can provide guidance, answer your questions, and offer assistance regarding travel-related concerns.

Coast Guard: +356 2123 8790
If you find yourself in an emergency situation at sea or require assistance related to maritime issues, you can contact the Malta Coast Guard. Their contact number is +356 2123 8790. They are responsible for maritime search and rescue operations and can provide assistance in emergencies.

It's important to keep these emergency contact numbers easily accessible. Save them in your phone, write them down, or have them readily available in case of emergencies. Additionally, familiarize yourself with your location and surroundings, so you can provide accurate details when contacting emergency services.

Remember, in serious emergencies, always call the appropriate emergency services first. They are trained to handle urgent situations and can provide the necessary assistance promptly.

TRAVEL TIPS AND ADVICE

Planning a trip to Malta? Here are some travel tips and advice to ensure a smooth and enjoyable experience:

Research and Plan Ahead:
Before your trip, research the attractions, activities, and cultural aspects of Malta. Familiarize yourself with the local customs, traditions, and basic phrases in Maltese. Create an itinerary that suits your interests and allows for exploration of both popular tourist spots and off-the-beaten-path destinations.

Best Time to Visit:
The best time to visit Malta is during the spring (April to June) and autumn (September to November) when the weather is pleasant, and the tourist crowds are smaller. Summers (July and August) can be hot and crowded, while winters (December to February) are mild but can be rainy.

Pack Accordingly:

Malta has a Mediterranean climate, so pack lightweight, breathable clothing for the summer months and layer up during the cooler seasons. Don't forget essentials such as sunscreen, a hat, comfortable walking shoes, and a swimsuit for beach visits.

Stay Hydrated:

The Mediterranean sun can be intense, so drink plenty of water to stay hydrated, especially during outdoor activities and sightseeing. Carry a reusable water bottle and refill it as needed.

Stay Safe:

Malta is generally a safe destination, but it's always wise to take precautions. Keep your belongings secure, be aware of your surroundings, and avoid walking alone in poorly lit or secluded areas at night. In crowded areas, be mindful of pickpockets and keep an eye on your belongings.

Public Transportation:

Public transportation in Malta is reliable and efficient. Buses are the main mode of transportation, and a single ticket can be used for multiple journeys within a specified time period. Taxis and ride-sharing services are also available, but they can be relatively more expensive.

Respect Cultural Norms:

Respect the local customs and traditions while visiting religious sites, such as churches and temples. Dress modestly, speak softly, and avoid disruptive behavior. Remember to seek permission before taking photographs of locals or inside religious premises.

Try Local Cuisine:

Maltese cuisine is diverse and delicious. Don't miss the opportunity to try local specialties such as pastizzi (flaky pastries filled with ricotta or mushy peas), rabbit stew, and ftira (Maltese bread filled with various ingredients). Visit local markets and restaurants to savor the authentic flavors of Malta.

Stay Connected:
Check with your mobile service provider regarding international roaming plans or consider purchasing a local SIM card for internet access and local calls. Wi-Fi is widely available in hotels, cafes, and public areas.

Travel Insurance:
Ensure you have comprehensive travel insurance that covers medical expenses, trip cancellation, and any other unforeseen circumstances. It's better to be prepared for any emergencies that may arise during your trip.

Respect the Environment:
Malta's natural beauty should be preserved. Respect the environment by disposing of waste properly, avoiding littering, and following any designated rules or regulations in protected areas.

Learn Basic Phrases:

Although English is widely spoken, learning a few basic phrases in Maltese, such as greetings and thank you, can go a long way in showing respect and connecting with the locals.

By following these travel tips and advice, you can make the most of your visit to Malta and create lasting memories of this beautiful Mediterranean destination.

CHAPTER 9

CONCLUSION

As your journey through this comprehensive travel guide to Malta comes to an end, it's time to reflect on the remarkable experiences that await you in this enchanting Mediterranean gem. Malta's captivating blend of history, culture, natural beauty, and warm hospitality offers a truly unique travel experience.

From the ancient temples of the Megalithic era to the medieval fortresses and baroque architecture, Malta's rich history is a testament to the countless civilizations that have shaped its identity. Exploring the fortified city of Valletta, wandering through the narrow streets of Mdina, and discovering the vibrant towns of Sliema and St. Julian's will transport you to a world steeped in tradition and heritage.

The natural wonders of Malta are equally captivating. With its crystal-clear turquoise waters, hidden coves, and picturesque beaches, the archipelago beckons sun-seekers and water enthusiasts alike. Snorkeling or diving in the vibrant underwater world, embarking on boat trips to stunning coastal formations, and exploring the rugged countryside through hiking trails offer endless opportunities for outdoor adventures.

Malta's culinary scene is a delightful fusion of Mediterranean flavors, blending traditional Maltese dishes with influences from neighboring countries. Indulge in the mouthwatering pastizzi, sample freshly caught seafood, and savor the unique flavors of local wines and craft beers. Visiting local food markets and experiencing the vibrant atmosphere of food festivals will immerse you in the gastronomic delights of Malta.

Beyond its tangible attractions, Malta embraces a vibrant cultural scene that manifests in festivals, events, and art exhibitions throughout the year. Witness the grandeur of traditional processions and revel in the spirit of lively celebrations. Explore museums and art galleries that showcase Malta's rich artistic heritage, and immerse yourself in the captivating world of Maltese folklore and traditions.

Throughout your journey, the Maltese people, known for their warm hospitality and friendly nature, will make you feel welcome. Embrace the local customs and etiquette, learn a few words in Maltese, and engage with the locals to forge meaningful connections and gain a deeper understanding of the Maltese way of life.

As you bid farewell to the picturesque landscapes, ancient ruins, and vibrant cities, take with you the memories of a destination that effortlessly combines the old and the new, the natural and the man-made. Malta's charm, beauty, and rich heritage will leave an indelible mark on your travel experiences.

Whether you seek historical wonders, idyllic beaches, thrilling adventures, or a cultural immersion, Malta offers it all. Let this travel guide be your companion, guiding you through the wonders of Malta and helping you create unforgettable memories in this captivating Mediterranean haven.

Printed in Great Britain
by Amazon

36527943R00126